THE HISTORY OF BARBOURNE

Claire Wardle

Terry Wardle

THE HISTORY OF BARBOURNE

and the early development of north Worcester

By Claire and Terry Wardle

*Eleven hundred years of recorded
history of Worcester's northern suburb*

*Published by
MTC Ltd*

Published 2007 by

MTC Ltd
PO Box 665
Worcester WR1 3WN

© Claire & Terry Wardle 2007

ISBN No: 978-0-9553809-0-7

Cover picture : Barbourne Road
about 1900. Courtesy of Ron Shuard.

CONTENTS

Preface

The history of Barbourne has never been written before, perhaps because local researchers felt it was simply a Victorian suburb of no particular interest over so many other suburbs which sprang up in the nineteenth century. Our research has shown however, that the area has a recorded history stretching back more than 1100 years, during most of which it was quite separate from the city of which it now forms part, so it seems to us that Barbourne's story is well worth telling.

We have attempted only a general survey of the history of the area up to about 1945 in this publication. For those who might wish to take aspects of this research further there is plenty of work remaining to be done. Since this book has no pretence to being a scholarly work there are no footnotes or lists of further reading, but anyone wishing to expand on aspects of our research will find the sources they need in the text or in the various archives listed in acknowledgements.

In many instances, where shops or businesses have gone, we have tried to indicate what is there now, but since shops and businesses continue to change hands this is something of a moving target. We therefore have to beg the indulgence of readers if names or uses have changed again since our research was done.

Not everyone interested in history shares the same tastes in periods and events so we have attempted to divide the book in a way which should offer something for everyone. Those readers who share an interest in the ancient history of the area will find what they want in the first part of the book, while those whose interest is in understanding how the modern suberb has been created can skip straight over to Part Two.

We have also put material on buildings, businesses and aspects of life in nineteenth and early twentieth century Barbourne into separate sections, so people will hopefully find what they want quickly and easily. We have grouped illustrations with relevant text so Parts Three and Four are mainly the places to go for those people whose interest is in old photographs, of which we have collected together as many as we could of Barbourne in the past, including a number never previously published.

Claire and Terry Wardle
Worcester
August 2006

Acknowledgements

Anyone who has tackled a research project such as this will know only too well how much reliance has to be placed on the information professionals who provide access to many of the research materials. Of those who have assisted in this case, thanks are especially due to the staffs of the Worcestershire Local History Centre; the Worcestershire County Record Office; Worcester City Archaeology; the Worcestershire Archaeology Service; Birmingham Central Library; the Codrington Library at All Souls College, Oxford and the British Library.

Thanks are also due to Worcester historian and collector Ron Shuard for generously giving his time and the benefit of his local knowledge and use of his research on the girls' grammar school; to archaeologist John Hemingway for allowing us to see his research on Anglo-Saxon Worcestershire; to Madeleine Goodier for information on her research into Barbourne Nurseries; to the Venerable Frank Bentley, Chaplain of St Oswald's; to David A. Attwood for permission to use his index of city planning applications which was valuable in helping to trace development in Barbourne during the period 1865 - 1900; to Jones bootmakers of Worcester and Barker shoes of Northants for assistance with leather processing queries; to Alice Ottley School and the Royal Grammar School Worcester; to Ian Pattison, churchwarden of St George's Church, for much help with church and parish matters; to Laurence Harper for assistance with property information relating to early twentieth century Barbourne; to Mike Grundy, whose popular historical columns have appeared in the Worcester News over many years, for generously giving his time and assistance; to Emma Hancocks of Worcestershire Archaeology for valuable help in mapping the bounds of Anglo-Saxon Barbourne; to Betty Johnson for thoroughly proof reading the manuscript; to all those people who helped us with information on their families and local businesses, whose names are included in the text; to the many authors, past and present, whose works we have consulted, and to all those people who kindly made time to talk to us about their memories of a Barbourne long past, as well as to anyone who has given us assistance during the long research process but whose name has inadvertently been omitted from these acknowledgements.

For assistance with or permission to use illustrations we are indebted to Worcester City Museums & Art Gallery, The British Library, Ron Shuard, Clive Haynes, John Hemingway, Ian Pattison, Martin Smith, John Smith, Jean Glover, Gladys Green, Brian Hewlett, Linda from Lee Design, Hallmark Solicitors, Mike Grundy and the Worcester News, the Co-operative Society, Jane Booth, Herefordshire Council, Worcester City Council, Ordnance Survey, Worcestershire Archaeological Society and HarperCollins Publishers. All rights remain with owners of the material.

Where, in some cases, it has not proved possible to trace or contact rights holders, we trust they will not object to our use of their material in the cause of illuminating Barbourne's past.

A draft of parts of this book was produced originally for sale to people taking part in a local history walk in Barbourne on Sunday 22 August 2004 in aid of the National Endometriosis Society and the SHE Trust. We are grateful to everyone who attended that event, not only for the queries raised, which prompted us to do additional research, but also for the intense interest they showed, which prompted us to believe that a book on the history of Barbourne might attract a readership.

Finally our thanks go to Marianne Wardle for constant help and encouragement, aid in research and much more assistance without which this book could never have been written.

Introduction

Where is Barbourne? That might sound like an odd question with which to begin a history of the area, but a problem we encountered early on is that it is not always entirely clear where Barbourne actually is. According to many modern maps of the city, Barbourne is hovering somewhere around the junction of the Droitwich and Ombersley Roads, which doesn't seem quite right, and seems to have sprung originally from the practice of showing the name 'Barbourne House' at this point.

Even the city council doesn't seem to know exactly where it is. No doubt they know where it is when they want to send out your council tax bills, but whilst doing this research we phoned to ask them where exactly they feel Barbourne is, and were surprised to find that they don't have a specific definition. "It depends what it's for," was the answer we got. Apparently for some purposes they might decide Barbourne continued some way up the Droitwich and Ombersley roads, for others they wouldn't. So there is no exact definition of what area Barbourne covers, though it is interesting that the area which many people today think of as the bounds of Barbourne, stretching almost equally south and north from the brook, has a good deal in common with the area it covered in Anglo-Saxon times.

The city council does have a sort of rule of thumb to define Barbourne, which highlights another odd thing about the area. At the other end of the city we have the London Road which goes to London, or at least in that direction, and the Bath Road which goes towards Bath, while at this end we have the Droitwich Road which goes in the direction of Droitwich, the Ombersley Road going towards Ombersley and we have the Barbourne Road which you might think would go towards Barbourne - but of course it doesn't. Broadly speaking the Barbourne Road, which runs from Little London to the Droitwich/Ombersley Road junction, *is* Barbourne and until the late nineteenth century it was just called Barbourne; the 'Road' being added first in a street directory of 1896. How far Barbourne extends back from the main road seems to be anyone's guess, but a reasonable assumption is that it takes in all the area between the river and the canal.

In this account we are going to take the city council approach and allow some flexibility in defining Barbourne because it is not possible to look at the early history of the area without looking at some developments which do not fall within the Barbourne Road area. And because Barbourne is only a part, albeit the most important part, of the story dealt with here of the development of the north of the city of Worcester, we will also cast the occasional glance at developments further afield. In this, we are perhaps in line with ancient practice since our study of the bounds of Anglo-Saxon Barbourne suggests that it extended much further to the north than the area does today.

PART ONE
EARLY HISTORY

The Distant Past

Very little is known of what was going on in this area in the earliest days of human occupation of Worcestershire. Much of the county would have been covered in dense forests which were the haunt of wolves and wild boar, but Barbourne, situated as it was on the pleasant riverside gravel terraces of the Severn valley, should have been an attractive site for permanent settlement by early farmers.

Barbourne Brook, which rises from a spring a few miles to the northeast beyond Perdiswell, would have meandered through the area much as it does today; the Severn would have followed much the same course to the west and the proximity of these two waterways makes it very likely that Barbourne was an area of early settlement - but not a pottery sherd of archaeological evidence has yet come to light to confirm this.

This is all the more frustrating since archaeologists have discovered proof of early occupation a little further south. Excavations along Loves Grove in 1993 produced evidence of what was thought to be prehistoric farming.

Seven years later, on the site of the new magistrates court in Castle Street, evidence was found suggesting a small settlement of late Iron Age round houses, which continued in use until the first or second century, and must have been the homes of the people farming in Loves Grove.

It is frustrating that we do not have this sort of information in relation to Barbourne, but these archaeological discoveries, and others from Roman times, resulted from excavation opportunities afforded by building developments, and no comparable developments have taken place in Barbourne.

The only early evidence attributable to Barbourne is a Neolithic oval stone scraper, reportedly in the possession of Worcestershire naturalist F.T. Spakman in 1907, which was said to have been found on the site of a former fever hospital standing at the junction of Pitchcroft Lane and Barbourne Walk.

Even if this stone tool had lain on the site since prehistoric times that is no proof of occupation, since it is the sort of thing that might easily have been dropped there by a passing Neolithic hunter. It might also have been discovered elsewhere by a Victorian collector and left or lost there, and since we have no way now of checking its age or origins it is really of no use to us as evidence.

Barbourne's distant past is therefore still shrouded in mystery, and is likely to remain so until opportunities arise for further detailed archaeological investigation of the area.

Roman Barbourne

The first evidence of human occupation in the area comes from the Roman or Romano-British period, and nineteenth and twentieth century archaeological finds enable us to paint a lively, if somewhat impressionistic, portrait of a thriving farming and industrial area with its own distinctive character.

The area also produced the first evidence of Roman occupation in the vicinity of Worcester. It was discovered in Britannia Square in 1829, during excavations to create the basement of Springfield, the large house in the centre of the square which is now part of Alice Ottley School. What workmen found was the base of a sandstone tower about 30 feet in diameter, and though only the foundations remained, their Roman origin seemed to be confirmed by a hoard of about 50 Roman copper coins from various reigns up to about 350 AD.

Worcestershire-born solicitor and antiquary Jabez Allies, who published the first book on British, Roman and Saxon antiquities in Worcestershire in 1852, examined the coins and may even have seen the foundations or certainly talked to people who had.

He decided the building must have been one of the series of forts known to have been built along the Severn by Ostorius Scapula while campaigning in this still relatively wild area around AD 50, just seven years after the Roman invasion. Presumably he thought the circular structure was a corner or 'curtain' tower of a fort.

Fifty years later an 'expert' writing in the Victoria County History, without seeing either the coins or the foundations, described Allies' theory as "gratuitous fiction" and in 1969 it was suggested that the circular structure was actually a temple.

'Springfield' in the centre of Britannia Square, where remains of a high status Roman villa were found when the cellar was being dug out in 1829.

So who was right? Sadly not Allies, whose theory might have made the Barbourne area the original military settlement from which Worcester had grown. Further excavations in the grounds of Springfield in the 1990s produced a range of Roman finds, which suggested not a fort but a high status building with columns, a hypocaust system and tiled roof; in other words, an out of town villa, which might well have had its own temple.

This evidence seems conclusive, though we have to remember that no-one has seen those circular foundations below the basement of Springfield since 1829, and since it is likely that they were taken up then, there is no chance of them being investigated further.

Nor can the coins be examined. They were said to have been presented to the Worcestershire Natural History Museum of that time and in 1901 were reportedly in the Worcester Museum, but staff tell us that they are not there now, nor in the county museum, and their current whereabouts are not known. Roman and Greek coins were also found at White Ladies in 1842 but this was later exposed as a hoax.

There is an interesting link between the Britannia Square coin hoard and evidence produced by excavations at The Butts in Worcester in summer 2003, which revealed some of the city's earliest Roman remains, dating from the 1st century AD through to the fourth century. Amongst the items found there were also coins from about 350 AD, and signs of burning on much of the material suggest that Roman Worcester may have shared the fate of many settlements when Picts, Scots and Saxons joined forces in 367 to sack south and central England. Presumably this area was abandoned for a time and maybe someone at the villa in what was to become Britannia Square left in too much of a hurry to pick up their hidden savings, or the villa petty cash.

The four centuries of Roman control of Britain seem to have been good ones for the settlement to the north of the city. Presumably the local tribes were quickly defeated or seduced by the advantages of the Roman lifestyle, and a mix of industry and high status housing spread north from the first century onwards.

Excavations in the 1990s have revealed evidence suggesting a large stone building of early Roman date on the Kardonia site at the Castle Street end of Farrier Street, a Roman domestic compound on the site where the police station now stands in Castle Street, with a possible gravel quarry nearby, possible signs of a pottery industry on the site of a former timber yard in Loves Grove and two high status Roman town houses in Moor Street.

The dominant building in the area must have been the villa in Britannia Square since the discovery in 1999 of foundations of another Roman building in the southern corner of the square, some distance from Springfield, presumably implies a substantial villa compound. If so this could have been the out of town residence of some senior local Roman official, or even a Romano-Briton who had prospered in trade, but such a large villa would have needed to be served by its own agricultural community, so it is likely that Barbourne provided the farming community which supported the villa and then, as later, Barbourne's rich soil was the key to the character of life in the area.

The industrial focus of life in Barbourne was a substantial iron working industry based along the Severn, on what is now Pitchcroft. The iron ore would have been brought in by river, possibly from the Forest of Dean, and smelted with wood from the adjacent forests in small, brick-lined, blast furnaces fed air through a footpump. The iron ingots could then be shipped out by river.

There must have been many of these blast furnaces spurting smoke and sparks into the sky night and day along Pitchcroft to judge by the substantial amounts of slag found not only there but on sites all over the city where it was probably used for infilling by builders in later centuries.

The industry was rediscovered by seventeenth century ironmaster Andrew Yarranton, the parliamentary governor of Hartlebury Castle during the civil war, who visited Pitchcroft, perhaps when he was in the city during one of the battles of Worcester, and noted "the hearth of a Roman footblast" and some Roman coins in an urn nearby. There were such substantial quantities of slag buried beneath Pitchcroft, in the area where the racecourse is now situated, that one elevated part of it was known as Cinder Point. For at least a decade from 1652, Yarranton shipped "many thousands of tons" of slag up the Severn for resmelting in his own more efficient blast furnace at Astley, near Bewdley, but signs of the Roman industry were to be seen for many years after. In 1796 local historian, Valentine Green, reported a Worcester physician, Dr Johnson, had told him that burnt bricks, "like the vestige of an iron furnace", were to be seen at low water, and as late as the 1840s antiquary Jabez Allies reported seeing slag six feet deep along the riverbank at Cinder Point, 200 - 300 yards from the city wall.

Despite the relatively large population suggested by all this activity no archaeological evidence has yet come to light of Roman burials in the Barbourne area. The nearest we have is some evidence suggesting an early barrow at Perdiswell. The evidence comes partly from an old field name, Barrow Cop, north of Checketts Lane, but the connection is by no means certain, stemming largely from the discovery of an incomplete but impressive bronze and iron torc in the adjoining field in 1840. A torc was a collar, necklace or bracelet, usually of precious metal, much favoured by ancient Britons and Gauls. This one was later acquired by antiquary Jabez Allies, who described it as eight inches long, weighing half a pound, from a finished length of probably 18 inches. An iron rod ran through the centre of twenty twisted and tooled pieces of bronze and between each pair was a thick ring.

The torc was exhibited to some interest at what was referred to as the Society of Antiquities (probably the Society of Antiquaries) in London in 1844. Allies suggested that this might well have been part of the grave goods from the barrow, but by then that feature had long since been levelled, probably during gravel extraction, and the little information we have suggests it was more typical of Celtic tribal burials than those of Roman Britain.

The Ancient Saltway

Though salt exploitation was doubtless an ancient industry, it was not until the arrival of the Romans that we get the first evidence of exploitation of salt at nearby Droitwich, which placed Barbourne on the ancient saltway to Worcester, whence salt cargoes were shipped down the Severn. There was also a salt house by the Severn at the end of what is now Lavender Road in Victorian times.

Other than Nantwich in Cheshire, Droitwich, called Saltwich by the Anglo-Saxons, was the sole source of industrial production of the mineral, which was so vital in food preservation and as a disinfectant, that Roman soldiers received a salt allowance or salarium as part of their pay, hence our modern word salary.

A charter of 717 shows that the Anglo-Saxons had revived the trade before that date and salt continued to be carted through Barbourne to the Severn for more than a thousand years. Attempts were made in 1655 and 1680 to create a water route from Droitwich to the Severn, but it was not until March 1771 that a canal was completed to the river at Hawford and salt cargoes began to bypass Worcester. Castle Street was used as a route to the river avoiding city tolls and was known as Salt Lane until it was renamed early in the nineteenth century, with the opening of the new county goal there which was built, for reasons best known to the architects, in imitation of a medieval castle; hence the new street name.

Today Birmingham-bound commuters daily hurry along the road north out of Worcester, unaware of the history they are passing, which is ironic when you consider that in the early days of the ancient salt route Barbourne was possibly bigger and certainly more important than the Birmingham of those far-off days.

Anglo-Saxon Barbourne

The recorded history of Barbourne as a distinct area really begins with the Anglo-Saxons. These European invaders had largely displaced the original inhabitants and taken control of the Severn valley by the beginning of the seventh century. Worcester was well established as an Anglo-Saxon settlement by the 660s and had its first bishop by about 679, but Barbourne was still some way outside the city and was to remain so for many centuries.

Ancient records identify the Saxons living near Barbourne Brook as the

Ludadingas. They were named in tribal records and their farmstead was referred to in a charter at the beginning of the tenth century. An Anglo-Saxon named Ludad was the original leader of this group; the name Ludadingas means 'Ludad's people'. They are described as a small tribe but were most likely an extended family, or several related families, possibly of as many as 30 or 40 or more people in all. They were one of many such small tribes or extended family groups throughout Worcestershire, who were brought together in the sub-kingdom of Hwiccia, which was originally part of the kingdom of Mercia to whose king, Penda, they paid tribute.

Later the Ludadingas found themselves paying the bishop instead, after someone - not Penda, since he wasn't a christian - gave the land to the church. This was quite common, and the church at Worcester grew fat on endowments in return for which priests were perpetually to pray for the souls of their late benefactors. Were the Ludadingas Christians when they found themselves paying their tribute to the bishop? It's hard to say. Mercia nominally became Christian in 655 when Penda died and was succeeded by his son Paeda, who had become a Christian two years earlier and married the daughter of the Christian king of Northumbria. But no doubt people in rural areas clung to their traditions and a reference to the old sacrificial god Tiw, who was linked to waterways and swamps, has been found in at least one place name in Worcestershire, though not in Barbourne.

The Ludadingas must have been among the first waves of Anglo-Saxon settlers, who obviously took the best land available, since their land at Barbourne was ideal for a settlement. Such settlements had to be self sufficient in food supplies, for which they needed good arable land to grow the corn which was the staple of Anglo-Saxon diet, 'mead-land' on the damp ground near rivers and brooks, which was vital to grow hay for winter feed for the cattle which were not slaughtered in the autumn, ley or rough pasture for summer grazing and woodland for timber, hunting game and pasturing the free-roaming herds of pigs from which came much of the wealth of people in Worcestershire at that time.

Barbourne had all this in abundance. Not just one watercourse but two, plus mead, ley, arable land and wooded higher ground. The Anglo-Saxons who settled here would have had to work hard but they must have had a comfortable life, farming on cleared forest land, fishing in the river, hunting and gathering in the forest margins and culling the herds of forest swine every autumn, literally bringing home the bacon to hang and smoke above the open fire in their simple rustic homes.

Though we have no way of knowing exactly what their life was like, we can get a picture from details of charters in other areas of Worcestershire. The boundaries and landmarks included in these charters were sometimes natural features such as streams, springs or even badger holes, but we also get references to man-made features such as hedges, ditches, crop fields and roads, suggesting that this was no wild wilderness but a rural landscape not too far from what we see in the countryside today. We even have a reference in a Claines charter to a "Made road" running to the town market, which must surely be the main road running through Barbourne, possibly a well made legacy of Roman times, on which salt and other cargoes, and people would travel through the settlement into Worcester.

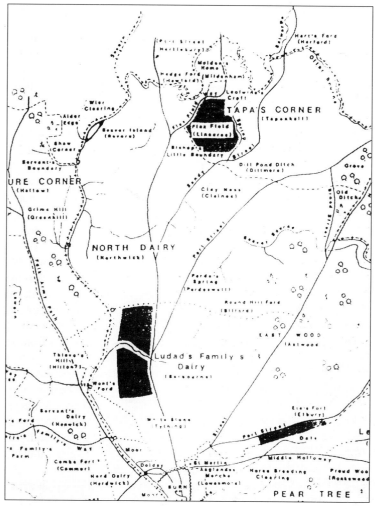

North Worcester in Anglo-Saxon times.
Courtesy of John Hemingway.

As to their home life we can offer nothing but speculation. We know the Anglo-Saxons were a social people with a love of storytelling and no doubt people gathered around the hearth, as they did in many Anglo-Saxon communities, to tell epic tales of gods and heroes, monsters and battles. They were people with a strong sense of their own past and though they had to rely on an oral tradition of history they could probably often recite their family tree for generations past.

Where did they live, these Ludadingas who inhabited Barbourne from the seventh century or earlier until at least the tenth century and probably until the coming of the Normans and afterwards? There is no archaeological evidence, so we have no clear answer and can only reason from the few facts we know. The Ludadingas must have had farm buildings associated with their dairy herd near the brook, but it would not have been a good place to live, let alone to store hay and grain, since the land around the brook regularly flooded from time immemorial and was also inclined to be marshy until the bed of the brook was concreted in the 1920s.

A better location would have been on the rising ground to the north, along the present Ombersley Road, and the most likely site is at the junction of the Ombersley and Northwick roads where there is a property called Barbourne Grange. Grange is an ancient name for a granary or farm and it is very possible that the site had that name long before the present Georgian house was built, probably in the late eighteenth century, and was the place where the Ludadingas built their homes and a granary for their hay and corn. Barring forestation, the Ludadingas would have had an excellent view from there down to the pastures along the brook.

Barbourne Grange

8.

About 794, according to A.E.E. Jones, the 1950s historian of Anglo-Saxon Worcester, a white stone was erected by an earl named Wilfrith near to Barbourne Brook. This was probably an estate or manorial boundary marker and may have led to the old name of the Tything hamlet, Tything Whitestones or Whitstones or Whistones; there seem to have been a number of versions of the spelling.

This name has more often been attributed to a later chapel on the Tything but in 1977 the Rev Douglas Beard, writing the history of the Tything parish and church of which he had been vicar for more than 40 years, was convinced that Wilfrith's marker, which he located near to St Oswald's, was the origin of the name. Certainly the name is very ancient, the area having formed part of the Northwick manor before 1218, when it was named as one of the tythings of the new parish of Claines, and it would make sense, given later boundaries, that white stone markers at St Oswald's and Barbourne Brook might have denoted the area as a manorial holding, at least until after the Conquest. So Wilfrith's white stones may be more likely to have given rise to the name than a medieval chapel whose provenance may anyway have been doubtful, as we will see later.

Despite the apparent prosperity of the calm rural life of Barbourne, people were still at the mercy of nature if crops failed or natural disasters occurred. These were a rural people with no welfare state to fall back on when times were hard. To some extent there were hard times every year, in the 'hungry gap' between the last of the old harvest and bringing in the new, but there were always the years people looked back on with a shudder.

Between 975 and 1051 there were at least seven of them for the Anglo-Saxons of Barbourne. Both 975 and 976 were years of great famine in England, ten years later disease killed many cattle, in 1005 came the worst famine that anyone could remember, nine years later flooding drowned many and destroyed settlements over a wide area, in 1041 bad weather destroyed crops, while a further outbreak of cattle disease killed much of the livestock, and on Sunday 1 May 1048 the Worcester monastic chronicler recorded that there was a "great earthquake" with "great mortality of men and cattle" affecting the whole area from Worcester to Droitwich.

As if these natural disasters were not bad enough, the people of Barbourne must have been caught up in the dramatic events of 1041 when Worcester was pillaged and lain waste, even though the village folk had nothing to do with the incident which caused these terrible events.

The incident was sparked by a repressive tax levied by the unpopular king Harthacanute, son of Canute. The people of the city rose against it, and though the king's two tax collectors took refuge in the monastery beside the cathedral they were seized and murdered. This enraged the king and he sent a powerful force to plunder and burn the city and kill all the inhabitants. Receiving word of this, the Worcester people fled to Bevereye, an island or sand bank in the Severn near present-day Bevere, and repulsed all attempts to dislodge them. The avengers had to content themselves with spending four days seizing anything they could find of value before firing the city as they left.

History doesn't record whether the folk of Barbourne were caught up in these events, but with an angry, avenging army in the area, furious at their inability to reach the inhabitants of Worcester on the Severn eye, no doubt the people of Barbourne would have been well advised to flee, either to the eye or the forest, until it was all over.

It is very likely that their homes were also destroyed and their livestock taken. Coming on top of the failure of crops in the bad weather of that year, this would have left the people of Barbourne in desperate straits and many must have died in the famine which would have followed.

Up to the start of the tenth century Barbourne had none of the status of larger recognised settlements such as Worcester, but at that point, for the very first time, we get a written record of its existence. It came in a charter made by Bishop Werferth of Worcester in the year 904, which showed that the Ludadinga farmstead was still in existence, and also gave a fascinating account of the character of the area.

The charter, reproduced in full at Appendix A, seems to be a response to the earlier generosity of Ethelred and his wife Ethelflaede, rulers of the kingdom of Mercia in which Worcestershire lay, in helping to restore Worcester after a damaging Viking raid. In response, the Bishop leased land both inside and outside the city, including Barbourne, to the Mercian rulers.

The land in the city was apparently the port area and a rectangular site behind it, which Worcestershire archaeologist John Hemingway has identified as stretching back from the Severn on the line of Bridge Street, since the present day Broad Street marks the line of the furthest northern expansion of Worcester in Anglo-Saxon times. Anglo-Saxon historian A.E.E. Jones said this area would have: "formed a bastion for Ethelred's military force controlling the passage of the river and the northern end of the city from the incursions of the Vikings".

The lease of land outside the city may have been intended to provide rents to help with the cost of manning this military bastion. The lands in Barbourne included the farmstead of the Ludadingas, who would now have a new landlord, and a total of 120 acres of arable land, split equally either side of Barbourne Brook.

The lease also included 12 acres of good meadowland, undoubtedly more of Pitchcroft, and more land on the other bank of the river taking in the county cricket ground, Cripplegate Park and the low-lying meadowland along Hylton Road. This substantial grant was made only for the lifetime of the Mercian rulers and their daughter, but it then got into the hands of the king and wasn't returned to the bishop until 972.

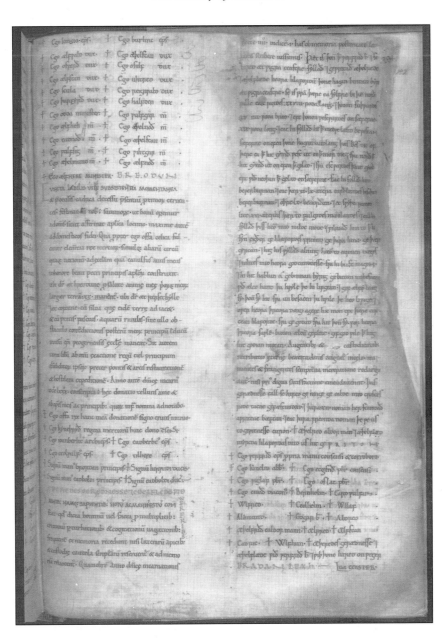

A copy of the 904 charter. Courtesy of the British Library.

11.

The picture this charter gives of life in the area is extremely valuable for historians of Worcester, but it provides an equally important insight into the life of early tenth century Barbourne. The Ludadingas, or their descendants, were clearly still in residence and were probably farming all of the 120 acres of arable land themselves since that was approximately the area of land thought necessary by the Anglo-Saxons to support a family. They were doubtless grazing cattle on the rich riverside pasture of what is now Pitchcroft. Interestingly there is no mention of woodland though there must have been some still on the higher ground to the north and east of the Ludadinga homestead; presumably the bishop kept this in his own hands.

It is not certain that the measures of the charter are equivalent to modern acres, but even so, a fascinating picture emerges when approximate acreages are planned on a modern map. Assuming that the boundaries were fairly straight, which of course may not have been the case, the 60 acres of arable land to the north of the brook would have had its south-eastern boundary where the brook comes close to the Worcester and Birmingham canal and its north-eastern boundary at the Bilford Road roundabout on Droitwich Road, on the edge of Perdiswell, with the northern boundary running roughly along the line of Coombs Road, Vine Street and Neweys Hill back to the river, which forms the western boundary.

This area beyond the brook takes in land from the northern end of Pitchcroft, across Gheluvelt Park and the former water works out to well beyond Northwick Avenue. stretching further north than we now suppose Barbourne goes, but there are still people living as far north as Northwick Road who regard themselves as being in Barbourne, and the northern boundary might well mark the southernmost extent of the ancient manor of Northwick, which had its heart further north at Old Northwick Lane.

To the south of the brook was another 60 acres of arable land, which would be very much the area covered by modern Barbourne. Its southern boundary is likely to have been at the bounds of the ancient Tything township, just to the south of Shrubbery Avenue, and it would have taken in almost all of Barbourne Road and all the land between the canal and the river, including the northern part of Pitchcroft.

The 12 acres of "good meadow land" referred to in the charter must have been the rest of Pitchcroft. This division of Pitchcroft into two separate parcels of land would explain why the two halves were two distinct land holdings until they were both given to the city by wealthy clothier Thomas Wylde in the sixteenth century.

One other fascinating fact which emerges is that Barbourne was referred to by the Anglo-Saxons as Beferburnan, which was later corrupted to its modern version. 'Burn' was Anglo-Saxon for a stream, clearly a reference to the brook, and 'befer' or 'bever', now spelt beaver, is a reference to those toothy, aquatic mam-

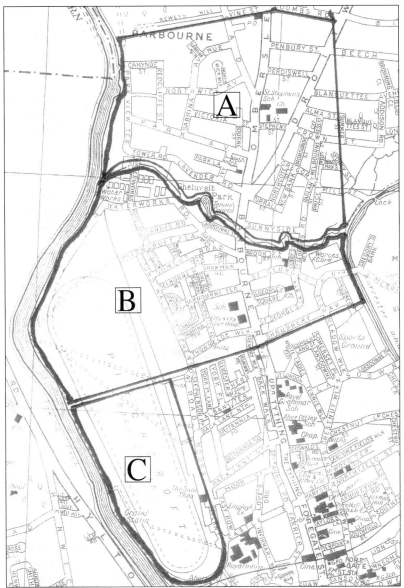

Anglo-Saxon Barbourne planned on a 20th century map. Areas A and B are 60-acre holdings of arable land while C is 12 acres of meadowland. There is no definite evidence of where the boundaries were and modern acres may not be equivalent to Anglo-Saxon, so this can only be an approximation of the boundaries of Barbourne in Anglo-Saxon times. Background map, from about 1950, courtesy of HarperCollins Publishers.

mals famous for building dams on rivers in the Canadian wilderness. Can these creatures have been frolicking in tenth century Barbourne Brook? We have no definite archaeological evidence, but the likelihood is that they were still here at that time, as they had been for centuries before. The beaver died out in England sometime in the medieval period, but still survives in Brittany.

One local tradition is that the weir at Bevere, which also owes its name to the beaver, being originally Bevereye, began as a beaver dam. It seems unlikely that beaver would have dammed the fast-flowing Severn, but the small weir at the bottom of Barbourne Brook might well have been a beaver dam originally.

The beaver would have formed part of the rich bounty of the land which doubtless gave early locals a happy life. Castoreum, a foul-smelling, bitter-tasting, reddish-brown substance secreted by the beaver, was valued as a cure-all as far back as ancient Greece, traditionally regarded as effective as an antiseptic for wounds and a treatment for rheumatism; also good for headaches presumably, since it contained salicylic acid, one of the main ingredients of aspirin.

Beaver would also have been hunted for their pelts for winter clothing, and their thick underfur, called felt, was used to make the fabric of that name, though it is now manufactured from synthetic fibres, chiefly in China. Probably the introduction of the first recorded mill on the brook in the late fourteenth century

The beaver gave Barbourne its name

was the beginning of the end for beaver in the area. Beaver damming the stream was the last thing the mill workers would have wanted, and the animals were probably exterminated as soon as possible.

Sadly, after the charter of 904, Anglo-Saxon Barbourne and the Ludadingas disappear from the written record. Barbourne was not a manor in its own right at that time, and though the land must have been included in the great Domesday survey of 1086 it is impossible to identify. We therefore have no information on the Anglo-Saxons who actually worked the land in Barbourne at this time, but if the Ludadingas or their descendants were still here after the conquest, which they surely must have been, they may have fared better than many Anglo-Saxons robbed of their rights by incoming Normans, since their landlord was then the great Bishop Wulstan, who alone amongst Anglo-Saxon prelates retained his see after the conquest.

Probably when the king returned the land in the 904 charter to the bishop in 972 it was incorporated into the bishop's manor at nearby Northwick, of which it formed a part in the early twelfth century. The bishop had substantial land holdings in Worcestershire and elsewhere, in addition to a third part of the revenue from the city of Worcester and many houses there, but Northwick was his main manor and the site of his manorial court, where tenants came to perform service. The heart of the manor is marked by the small green on Northwick Road at the junction with Old Northwick Lane which runs down to an ancient river crossing, but it included Beferburn or Barbourne, Bevereye or Bevere, Tapenhall, Claines, Astwood, Mildenham with Hawford, Smite with Tolladine, Whistones and Tibberton. The manorial title subsequently became Northwick and Whistones and later Claines after a new parish church was built there.

From 1218 Barbourne became part of the large new parish of Claines, stretching from the city wall and the Severn to Ombersley in the north and Hindlip and Warndon in the east. The bishop later moved to Hartlebury and the lands of the old Northwick manor gradually came under secular control. The bishop's remaining holdings were transferred to the Ecclesiastical Commissioners in 1860.

Religious Houses

Strictly speaking there were no religious houses in Barbourne, but there were two close by, and the medieval history of the Barbourne area was closely connected with them. There are virtually no ancient remains of these houses today, nor any medieval plans to show what buildings they possessed, and what little we know of them therefore has to be deduced from their histories.

The earliest of these was the **Hospital of St Oswald**, one of the oldest charitable foundations in the country, reputedly established by Oswald himself while he was bishop from 962 to 991 and originally, according to a sixteenth century account, an isolation hospital for monks suffering from leprosy, which might suggest strong links with Europe since leprosy wasn't usually found in this country at that date. An elusive manuscript source, quoted by several early Worcestershire historians, reportedly showed that the original foundation was for a chaplain, a master and four brethren to care for the inmates.

A hospital was set up by Bishop Wulstan about 1085 in what is now known as the Commandery, but it was on the far side of the city beyond the Sidbury gate. The only other early hospital which existed in Worcestershire was St Mary's in Droitwich, not set up until 1285. Of the three, only St Oswald's has survived as a charitable institution. The exact date at which St Oswald's became a hospital is not known, but it must have been before 1268 when a benefactor left ten shillings "for the infirm of the hospital".

The other, probably better known, religious house was the convent known as **White Ladies**, about which there is a great deal of confusion. One twentieth century Worcester historian confidently asserts that the convent was originally beside the cathedral but the nuns were ungallantly evicted to the wild forests outside the city by St. Oswald in 969 to make way for monks, which doesn't sound like a very saintly thing to do. Another insists that White Ladies was the only nunnery ever founded at Worcester.

In fact there was an earlier convent in Worcester, referred to in a charter of 899, which was apparently presided over by Ethelburga, daughter of Alfred the Great, but the endowment was only for her lifetime and the convent seems to have ceased by the time Oswald was carrying out his reforms in 969, which involved persuading secular canons near the cathedral to become monks, not evicting nuns.

There was also a small body of Penitent Sisters in Worcester in 1240 but little is known of them.

The house at White Ladies, originally called the convent of St Mary Magdalene but quickly renamed in popular parlance due to the white habits of the nuns, was founded by bishop Walter de Cantilupe, probably soon after he became bishop in 1237.

The earliest known charter concerning the convent confirmed the nuns in possession of the site in 1255, but it must have been founded before then because

Remains of the White Ladies convent, pictured about 1835. Courtesy of Worcester City Museums & Art Gallery.

16.

in 1240 Henry III ordered the bailiffs of Tewkesbury to send the "White Sisters" a cask of his wine; perhaps a gift to help celebrate the opening of the convent. Work on the convent chapel was still going on in the following year when the king granted the sisters 10 oaks from the forest of Kinver and 100s for the building work.

White Ladies was part of the reform movement sweeping through the monastic establishment. During the earliest centuries of monastic settlement in Worcestershire the rule of St. Benedict had prevailed, and the intent of Oswald's tenth century reforms had been to strengthen Benedictine rule, but well endowed monasteries inevitably fell to arguing covetously over their possessions and neglecting their vocation, and thus the desire for change gave rise to the Cistercians, a proliferating reform movement within the Benedictine order, which set up a Worcestershire house near Redditch and, in the thirteenth century, two nunneries in the county, of which this was the first.

No original plan has survived of the buildings of the convent, but there are references to the buildings in later centuries which give us a fairly clear picture of what they comprised, if not exactly where they stood. The convent had a chapel dedicated to St Mary Magdalene, which was apparently ruinous by the 1540s, probably due to 'robbing out', when the buildings had become Whistone Farm. A surviving wall of the chapel, which forms part of an eighteenth century building on the site today, shows that the chapel was of red sandstone, as no doubt

Remains of the White Ladies convent chapel incorporated into later buildings on the Royal Grammar School site.

other convent buildings were. A crypt below the chapel was probably the burial place of prioresses.

The main range of buildings was of two storeys, described in the eighteenth century as having a multi-gabled roof and square-headed windows, though those were likely to have been a seventeenth century 'modernisation'. The refectory, which apparently incorporated the kitchen, was described as "a spacious and handsome apartment" and there was a panelled room above with a small chamber off, perhaps the living and sleeping quarters of the prioress. To the north of the convent buildings was a small burial ground and later a tithe barn. The priest of St Swithin's was engaged to minister to the nuns' spiritual needs and he was said to be still in receipt of the emolument in the mid-nineteenth century, long after the convent had closed!

The convent was not large in numbers, probably the average number of nuns in residence at any one time was about six, and it was never wealthy; in fact, says one source, its poverty was "proverbial". In 1275 Bishop Giffard pleaded that the nuns were barely able "to support their own needs, much less to pay heavy taxation," and in 1284 the bishop gave corn and barley and money to buy herrings for all the nuns "on account of their poverty". Many other such gifts are recorded over the years.

How did the poverty of the sisters become so well known? A document of 1308 from sub-prioress Lucy de Solers suggested they lost no opportunity to make it known. In a letter pleading they be let off some dues to the new bishop, she said the smallness of their possessions "compelled the nuns formerly to beg to the scandal of womankind and the discredit of religion". Lucy certainly had a way with words, and her ready phrases on "the honour of religion" and "the frailness of the female sex" no doubt persuaded many a wealthy churchman to part with gifts for the convent.

Over the centuries some small gifts made the nuns a little wealthier. In 1301 they received 12 acres of land and an acre of woodland in the bishop's manor of Northwick, which included Barbourne; another 20 acres came their way 30 years later and yet another 6 acres and half an acre of meadow in the following year. In 1331 Joan Talbot, widow of Sir Richard Talbot of Richard's Castle, near Leominster in Herefordshire, gave the nuns "one messuage (house and grounds), 15 acres of land, 1 penny rent and half an acre of meadow, with appurtenances", also in Northwick.

This must have helped, but it was very small beer compared to the vast possessions of the major monasteries and a royal grant in 1400 of £10 a year must have been very welcome, though an order from Henry VII to the sheriff in 1487 to pay all arrears suggests the sisters didn't see their money very often.

Who were these women who became 'White Ladies', and what did they do in the convent? Most of the nuns were probably not young women choosing a vocation rather than marriage and a family, but older ladies who were widowed after raising their children and chose to spend their remaining years in the relative calm of the convent, and despite the poverty of which the nuns complained, some were from quite wealthy, titled families.

Prioress Lady Agnes de Bromwich, who died in 1308, was succeeded by Lady Alice de la Flagge, prioress for 20 years, who was from a wealthy Claines landowning family. By some accounts, the land she brought to the convent stretched as far as Perdiswell, thus taking in Barbourne, and one piece of this land is still known as Flag Meadow, and is used today as a school sports ground. St George's Lane was known originally as Flag Lane, suggesting that the parcel of land gifted to the convent by Lady Alice certainly stretched much further than Flag Meadow Walk. The nuns also owned 53 acres in the ancient manor of Estun or Aston which became linked in name to them as White Ladies Aston, and they are also remembered by their Nunnery Farm at Whittington and Nunnery Wood.

Sadly we have almost no information on what the nuns did. It has been suggested that they founded the first school for girls in the area and, perhaps because of the proximity of the hospital, that they studied medicine and nursing, but there is no evidence for any of this. The only firm information we have, from a document of 1476, is that in return for their royal £10 a year the nuns would every Friday "goo a procession saying the lateneye for the tranquylite and peas of this roialme of England and remembryng our founder the bishop of Worcester in the same". Perhaps, given their habitual poverty, the nuns spent some of their time toiling on their land to grow their food.

Apparently the election of a new prioress could be a colourful break from routine. Lucy de Solers wrote a detailed account of the election of Alice Flagge, "a woman of discreet life and morals, of lawful age, professed in the nunnery, born of lawful matrimony, prudent in spiritual and temporal matters". It was apparently the fashion for the prioress-elect to profess a certain modesty about taking office, and Alice had to be led to her election "weeping, resisting as much as she could and expostulating in a loud voice, as is the custom".

Around 1536 the convent of the White Ladies ceased to exist when Henry VIII dissolved the minor monasteries and its lands were taken by the crown. Poor to the last, the total value of their possessions was £56 3shillings and 7pence, a fraction of the value of most monasteries. The last prioress, Jane Burrell, was given a pension of £5 10 shillings for a few years. Though little is known of their lives, nothing is known to the detriment of the nuns, which is more than can be said of their neighbours at the hospital.

Of the quality of their medical care we know little, but history has provided us with some intriguing accounts of the doings of the brothers at the hospital. In 1321 Bishop Cobham instructed Thomas Bromley, dean of Worcester and thus overseer of St Wulstan's hospital, to enquire into allegations that the brethren of

St Oswald's led dissolute lives and wasted the goods of the hospital. As a result of his investigation the master of St Oswald's, William de Claines, was removed from the job.

In 1394 the monks were again in trouble and the bishop ordered measures to "punish and correct the crimes and excesses of the master and brethren of the house of St Oswald". The master, William Bysseley, was forced to make a public confession and was replaced. At the election of Thomas Parker as master in 1454 additional provision was made to keep the brethren in order. Documents from this time suggest that misuse of land gifted to the hospital might have been part of the problem. This was to be a continuing source of trouble in following centuries.

The hospital had a chapel or church dedicated to St Oswald and a substantial graveyard also covering the area opposite, later occupied by Kays the catalogue company, which was said to have been created originally to cater for the victims of leprosy and those caring for them. What is now St Oswald's Road was originally a path through the graveyard, having been made into a road by 1874.

The graveyard at the cathedral was once the only other burial place in Worcester and St Oswald's was used to bury plague victims, either because the cathedral could not cope with the numbers or, perhaps more likely, because the citizens preferred to have the plague pits sited outside the city. Later it was used for the burial of strangers, victims of contagious diseases and criminals. Under the law of that time one of the latter was Jesuit Father John Wall, who was executed on Red Hill on 22 August 1679. His body lies somewhere near the west wall of the hospital where a commemorative plaque is fixed and there is also a memorial at the site of his execution, at the rear of No. 4 Whittington Road, to which there is public access.

The dissolution of the monasteries did not affect St Oswald's as it had the convent, because Nicholas Udal, who became master in 1538, quickly leased out all the hospital's lands for 99 years, thus avoiding them being seized by the crown. He recreated the hospital as almshouses, which was probably part of its role in past centuries and one which still continues today, but the hospitals of St Oswald and of St Wulstan at the Commandery were closed, and thus the Worcester area was left without a hospital for more than 200 years until the Infirmary first opened its doors in premises in Silver Street in 1745.

The Whitestones

Between St Oswald's hospital and White Ladies there was said to be an orchard in which stood, from an early date, a mortuary chapel attached to the hospital, at which mass was said daily for the rest of those buried in the hospital graveyard. The story goes that this was of white limestone, in contrast to the red sandstone previously used in the area, which led to the name of Tything Whitestones or Whistones, but it has already been noted that the original white stone may have been placed near Barbourne Brook in the eighth century as a boundary marker. 'Tything' does not seem to have been attached to the name of the area until after the convent tithe barn was built, which could not have been earlier than the second half of the thirteenth century, and it was only around that time that the name Wistan or Whytston first appears in records.

There is clear evidence that the hospital had its own chapel, so a separate mortuary chapel may have been of earlier date, but there is no evidence of this. It has been suggested that it served as a resting place for royal remains being taken to Worcester for burial at the cathedral and it was demolished in the time of Henry VIII.

The presence of a mortuary chapel would seem to suggest that the former orchard was being put to use as a part of the hospital graveyard but legend has it that this was an orchard in 1575 when a pear tree was taken from it and replanted on The Cross, from which Queen Elizabeth was famously said to have plucked the three pears which appear in the city arms. Planting, or re-planting, an orchard on ground used recently for burials would have been unthinkable to the hospital brethren, so it is probably more likely that the orchard lay behind the wayside chapel which must have fronted onto the main road.

It also seems odd that the hospital, which had only one chaplain and four brothers, should have had two chapels and it may be that the 'white stones' chapel was the one we know of at St Oswald's, but that was taken down in the sixteenth century not the fifteenth. So the legend of the chapel of white stones, said to have given the area its old name, is something of a mystery and, as we mentioned earlier, a white stone boundary or manorial marker or markers from the late eighth century is perhaps a more likely source of the old name, considering how ancient it is.

The Convent Tunnel

Another mystery. Legend has it that in olden days a tunnel led to White Ladies Priory from the cathedral so that there was a means of escape in case of attackers storming the city. This won't be a surprise to anyone who has spent time studying local history, because almost every town, city, village and manor house has a specious legend of a subterranean passage going somewhere or other. Many manor houses have tales of tunnels to the local pub so the lord of the manor could make his way there unseen, though local legends rarely explain why he would bother when everyone in the pub would see him, or for that matter, how he managed to crawl back through the tunnel when thoroughly inebriated. Even more colourful tales often attach to monasteries, suggesting the monks had a secret tunnel to the nearest convent. The occasional stately home did have a service tunnel to outlying buildings but these would only be short; nothing like the lengthy constructions of folklore. Usually these tales of lost tunnels were based on a modicum of reality - a drainage tunnel, cool underground food storage, etc. - and a good deal of imagination did the rest.

In this case though there apparently was something to the story. Eighteenth century Worcestershire historian Treadway Nash recorded that he had entered the tunnel in the Tything and proceeded about 100 yards before "foul air" caused his lantern to go out and he had to retreat. But in which directions was the tunnel going and how could Nash be sure that he had gone 100 yards? It's notoriously difficult to judge distance and direction underground. If the tunnel had been high enough for Nash to stand up he might have been able to pace out the yards in the time-honoured manner, but that is unlikely, and if he had to crawl, it would be impossible to judge the distance accurately. A tunnel all the way from the cathedral to Little London - and some sources suggest on to Hindlip - seems highly improbable, but Nash's experiment seems to show there was a tunnel going somewhere.

Worcester historian Bill Gwilliam records that "the tradition gathered strength" when The White Witch of Worcester, "a lurid piece of Victorian fiction set in the period of the Barons' Wars of the 13th century", was published by James Skipp Borlase in serial form in the Worcestershire Chronicle in the 1880s. Prior to this however, the British Archaeological Association met in Worcester in 1848 and made strenuous efforts to find the tunnel Nash had entered, but without success. A blocked arch at the south corner of the west wall of the chapel crypt, which was pointed out by elderly locals as the place where Nash had entered the tunnel, was thoroughly investigated, but no tunnel was found. A series of trenches were then dug in other likely spots, but with no greater success.

Unless Nash is to be regarded as a hoaxer, and certainly he had no such reputation amongst his contemporaries, we have to allow that there was some sort of underground passage in the area of the nunnery, but neither archaeological excavations nor later building foundations have uncovered it, and the claims of tunnels running for miles are bizarre to say the least. The tunnel could have been a 'service' access to the chapel from an outlying building, possibly the sleeping accommodation, but this seems an unlikely luxury for a poverty stricken convent. The most likely explanation therefore seemed to be that, like most such supposed 'tunnels', the White Ladies tunnel was either an underground storage facility or a drain of some sort, and there the matter rested for a century.

But this was one mystery which just would not go away, and during the preparation of this book we came across three reported 'sightings', apparently not known to city archaeologists, of the mysterious White Ladies tunnels. Two were reported to us by Miss Bridget Monahan who was born about 1910 and whose father was Rev William Beattie Monahan, rector of St Swithin's and old St Martin's churches for 46 years from 1902.

Miss Monahan recalls that signs of a tunnel were found near St Swithin's when buses began to replace trams and an old tram drivers' urinal and its associated sewage installation was being removed. A more definite sighting she reports was when road widening was taking place near what was then the Hopmarket Hotel.

The third sighting was north of White Ladies, perhaps suggesting there was, after all, a tunnel running on beyond the convent. During the second world war, Fred and Rose Shuard, uncle and aunt of Worcester historian Ron Shuard, opened a butcher's shop in a cottage on the corner of Little London opposite the site of the convent tithe barn, and when part of the living room floor subsided they saw beneath it what looked distinctly like the remains of a tunnel. So the mystery of whether there was really a White Ladies tunnel, or even tunnels, goes on into another century and is still unsolved.

Medieval Barbourne

The ordinary working people of Barbourne were undoubtedly worse off in the late eleventh century, after the Norman Conquest had brought in a harsh new aristocracy, than in the seventh century when they had the freedom of the woods, the fields and the river, though whether they were worse off than in the early eleventh century, just before the Conquest, is open to question,

Records of the post-Conquest period show a society where nothing was free, everything was for sale, though this may have been a trend which was perceivable in Anglo-Saxon England. Everything from woodland to river and mead had a price, and if you couldn't afford it you couldn't use it.

At least from the Conquest, and possibly earlier, the bishop held the fishing rights in the Severn which were granted to the Priory of Worcester in 1117. Mead, arable and woodland were all the domain of the bishop residing at Northwick, so no matter how hard times were there would be no chance to supplement your diet with game or fish, unless you were prepared to take the risk of poaching, for which punishment was severe. Gradually land ownership diversified as Worcester expanded and the bishop eventually moved his seat and main manor to Hartlebury.

The descent of Barbourne from church benefice to private holding can be traced through less than two centuries following the Conquest. It was almost certainly amongst lands granted to the ancestors of Robert de Theulf, bishop of

Worcester from 1115 to 1123. It was granted to Ralph de Wilington early in the thirteenth century, but it had formerly belonged to his father-in-law Robert de Evercy, who was presumably a descendant of the bishop.

It is unlikely that this land included the whole of Barbourne however; certainly it was not the end of church ownership of land in Barbourne, because from the thirteenth century documents show the bishop's manor of Northwick linked with Wistan or Whytston as one manor, which must surely have included Barbourne or parts of it.

The bishop had moved from Northwick before the dissolution and it is possible that Wistan had been functioning as a separate manor for some time, though still under the bishop's control. The prior of the monastery at Worcester also apparently held land in the area in the thirteenth century, since an Osbert de Barbourne gave knight's service to the prior in return for tenements he held in the area.

In 1539 the antiquary Leland refers to "a fayre manor house" by St Oswald's chapel "much repaired of late by one Parker, chancellor of the bishop of Worcester". This is the only reference made to a manor house in the Tything and the fact that the bishop's man was repairing it shows that it must have been there for some time and was still owned by the bishop, with Parker presumably as hospital master.

Where people in Barbourne worshipped and were married and buried in the earliest days is not clear, but possibly in a city parish. Claines was a chapelry to the parish of St Helens in the city until 1218, when it became a separate parish which continued to include Barbourne for almost six and a half centuries. The fact that Barbourne's parish church stood almost two miles away was to be a continuing problem over the centuries.

Thomas Habington, writing in the first half of the seventeenth century, said he had seen a document from 1378 showing that "in this township (Beareborn) were seven freeholders, the principal formerly the prior of Worcester and Prioress of the White Ladies and then also as many customary tenants". On Barbourne brook was a mill "buylded by William Frebara, Master of St Oswald's", and "below thys is Bearebourne's bridge, over which lyethe as greate a roade as most in thys shyre and where it (the brook) fallethe into Severne hathe aunciently byn a were".

This is a fascinating picture of late fourteenth century Barbourne and the brook which really led to its existence. It was most likely diverted and dammed when the mill was built, to create the race for the mill, which by this evidence was not far from the present Barbourne Road.

This mill, built about 1369 for grinding corn, was reputedly the forerunner of that later leased by Thomas Gregory, after which the area to the east became known as Gregory's Mill. The mill was still working during the First World War but closed shortly afterwards, faced with competition from more powerful steam-powered mills, and had been completely demolished by 1950.

The fact that the road was "as great as most in thys shyre" and that the brook had been bridged, probably with a timber bridge, is most likely a testament to the wealth created by the salt trade, and this seems to be confirmed by the fact that 60 years after the trade had by-passed Worcester there was only a footbridge over the brook while vehicles had to ford it.

Archaeological evidence, obtained in the early 1990s, shows that there was a layer of timber and brushwood forming a cordwood causeway approaching the medieval bridge at either end. The timbers were laid 0.75m apart on a bed of brushwood over grey sand which would have created a good all-weather approach to the bridge.

The salt trade must have brought considerable traffic to the road and it wouldn't be human nature if the people of Barbourne hadn't tried to profit from it by providing some services for the passing carters; the Swan Inn beside the brook is reputed to be descended from a hostelry of ancient foundation, though the present building is modern.

Habington's writing is also a fascinating example of how the name, and the English language, was developing during the early seventeenth century. In a relatively short piece of text, including a few phrases not quoted here, he spelt the name in three different ways: Beareborn, Bearebourn and Bearebourne.

We sadly have no detailed information about the mill and the form of its construction at that time, though there is a painting of it from the early nineteenth century, but this is nevertheless notable as the first definite reference to a building in Barbourne itself.

There must have been others; we can imagine the farm buildings of the Ludadingas and their successors and perhaps a roadside shelter which developed into an inn, but aside from the convent and hospital, which were beyond Barbourne proper, the only other building of which we have a clear report is a tithe barn for the tithes due to the convent, which stood at the corner of Little London on the site of the present almshouses. The ruins of the barn were taken down in the eighteenth century but the tithing has survived in the modern road name.

The sixteenth century dissolution of the monasteries and the seizure of their lands by the crown led to a 'feeding frenzy' in land sales and in 1543, seven years after the dissolution of the White Ladies Priory, the site and Barbourne, or at least the land that the White Ladies had held at Barbourne, passed into the hands of Richard Callowhill and remained in that family for some time.

In 1573 the convent site was granted to the Worcester free school, of which more later, but the Callowhill family and their descendants and other tenants continued to lease White Ladies, or Whiteladies as it was later styled, as a residence for the next 300 years.

St Oswald's after the Dissolution

Though the former hospital was saved from seizure by the crown during the dissolution, it suffered almost as badly from the depredations of those wealthy landowners through whose hands its leases passed in the following centuries. Masters of St Oswald's were often non-resident churchmen and the resultant lack of on-site scrutiny meant unauthorised felling of timber and gravel extraction thrived on its lands. Even the medieval hospital chapel disappeared.

One colourful story was that the lease came into the hands of "fervent catholic" Sir John Bourne, who demolished the chapel and used the stone for his house at Holt, telling those who challenged him that he would rebuild the church when the king restored "the true religion". It's a good tale, but Holt Castle was built in the fifteenth century not the sixteenth, and not by Sir John Bourne, who didn't buy the manor until the late 1550s.

That doesn't mean of course that he might not have demolished St Oswald's chapel and sold off the stone. Certainly he used chapel floor and roof tiles for repair work at Holt and he was accused of demolishing the chapel at the Court of Exchequer, but this accusation has to be seen against a background of strong anti-Catholic sentiment at that time. Whoever demolished the chapel did it thoroughly, and when prominent Oxford cleric Samuel Fell became master in 1631 he had to search for the foundations of the building in the overgrown churchyard.

One very odd report emerged from this period. Amid the ruins, said Habington: "weare lately found the bones of a man of extraordinary leangthe, being 13 foute and a halfe yet of lowe degree (as it seemed) for hee was buryed in the churchyard". Could there really have been a man of well over double the normal human height walking the lanes of Barbourne in those far off days? It seems more likely that what had been discovered were the bones of more than one man, which had been mistaken for a single burial, but Habington was adamant that this was the grave of just one man and he added that bones "of far greater leangthe and bygnes" had recently been discovered near Gloucester "within a coffyn of such rare pretious stone as I thincke scarce any Emperor had eaver the lyke".

Dr John Fell, son of Samuel, who became master of St Oswald's in 1665 after the civil war, and later Bishop of Oxford, found that the hospital buildings had suffered once more, this time at the hands of the combatants. He put out £450 of his own money, a considerable sum in those days, to provide a new house for St Oswald's where "eight poor men and two poor women were maintained".

Dr Fell was also Dean of Christ Church, Oxford, and is celebrated as the founder of the Oxford University Press and procurer of its excellent typefaces, which have continued to be known as the 'Fell types', but despite his achievements it is his sad fate to be remembered chiefly as the unfortunate subject of the undergraduate jingle:

> I do not love thee, Dr Fell;
> The reason why I cannot tell;
> But this I know and know full well,
> I do not love thee, Dr Fell.

Dr Fell's donation was supplemented in 1681 by local farmer Thomas Hayes or Haynes who provided six additional rooms or houses and £50 a year in a settlement under which ten poor men and one woman of at least 50 years of age were to be chosen by the mayor and two aldermen to occupy the hospital. They were to receive 2 shillings each a week, three tons of coal and every two years a "sad-coloured" garment, "down to the ankles".

Despite these examples of generosity, the hospital became a "cash cow" to generations of deans of Worcester who invariably profited greatly from appointing themselves as master of St Oswald's. In 1824 an investigation was launched into the management of Dean Jenkinson, a first cousin of the prime minister Lord Liverpool. He was infamous for holding numerous profitable ecclesiastical positions without carrying out any of the duties. Under his mastership of St Oswald's it was found that the endowments of the hospital had "almost disappeared".

The scandal that followed however did little to affect the dean, who died quietly at Malvern in 1840, but the ensuing court case lasted the best part of half a

St Oswald's about 1784

century. When the hospital finally recovered its property in 1875 its annual income went up from £450 to £20,000!

This was not good news for everyone however. The case centred around building leases on land between St Oswald's and Castle Street under which the lessees built shops and houses, but a smart lawyer spotted a defect in the leases and they were eventually withdrawn without compensation. 'Stroller', an anonymous columnist in the Worcester Herald and later Berrows Journal in the 1920s and 30s, recalled knowing a family affected by the case 70 years earlier, who, he said, had been reduced "from comparative affluence to poverty by this outrageous legal robbery".

In 1873, perhaps in anticipation of a positive result in the court case, rebuilding of the hospital began, to create the Victorian Gothic buildings we see today, which included 37 dwellings for 20 men and 17 women, and are said to be built in the same position as the original buildings, though it is clear from recent archaeological discoveries on the site that the seventeenth century chapel must have been somewhat to the west of the present building.

Though it was never a parish church, the hospital chapel opened its doors to the public and had acquired many of the functions over the centuries, and even a casual study of the gravestones and chapel memorials shows that with the development of a new fashionable suburb for Worcester's wealthy and powerful it became the centre of worship for many eminent citizens.

At the beginning of the twentieth century, before the advent of the welfare state, residents of the hospital received 8 shillings a week plus coal, and had just one room each. About 25 years ago the buildings were remodelled to create comfortable flats accommodating just over half the original number of tenants.

Today the possessions of the hospital are nothing like they once were, but in 1998 St Oswald's still owned the school playing fields and allotments which cover a good deal of the south side of Lansdowne Road, and retained an interest in a handful of properties in Foregate Street.

The first northern expansion of Worcester

In 1539 the antiquary John Leland visited Worcester and found "a lounge and fair suburbe by north without the Foregate and at the Northeast parte and very end of it is an auncient fayre large chappell of St Oswald".

His report proves that Worcester was expanding fast out of its medieval walls, which, by the twelfth century, had advanced only as far north as the Butts, but also that the hospital really marked the end of this first northern expansion and Barbourne, beyond the convent, still lay in the countryside. This suburb, developed on church land outside city control, might have looked good to Leland but it had grown quickly and just as quickly developed into slum housing for the poor, probably forsaking the safety of the walls in return for lower rents.

The Foregate in the medieval wall was situated where the Hopmarket now stands; city historian Hubert Leicester records seeing the foundations during construction of the Hopmarket Hotel, as it then was. Beyond this the city also controlled the land up to the 'liberty post' which was on the south side of Castle Street. The liberty posts were supposedly set a bowshot from the city walls, though it would have needed a good archer to shoot that far. By creating the saltway across the meadows to the river, immediately beyond the liberty post, the carters avoided the tolls charged when carts passed through the city gates.

The Foregate, Worcester's gateway to Barbourne, as reconstructed by early 20thC city historian Hubert Leicester.

The thoroughfare leading out of the city north to Barbourne was originally called Forest Street, which gives some idea of the continuing nature of much of the land to the north of the city. It was only much later, when the city began to extend north, that the name Foregate Street appeared and the area beyond Castle Street to Little London, where the tithe barn stood, became known as Tything Street.

Beyond the liberty post, the Tything of Whistones was said to have been an ancient township, but by the late fifteenth and early sixteenth centuries it was an unplanned jumble of tenements and hovels, a magnet for vagrants and migrants, for the poor and the lawless, since the area was beyond the jurisdiction of the city authorities. In the slums straggling along this important thoroughfare, the workshops of 'noisome' tradesmen, such as soap boilers and lime-burners, stood shoulder to shoulder with inns, unlicensed ale houses, brothels and cheap, lice-infested, lodging houses in a complex of ill-constructed and often temporary structures thrown up by unscrupulous sub-landlords; in 1635 one of these hovels was described as "no better than a pigscoat". The stench must have been almost unbearable. A typical tenement might be about 5 by 6 metres in size and that space would have to house a family and often also apprentices and even lodgers.

The overcrowding problems were caused by the massive growth in the population, with many poor people flooding into the area from Wales. The population of Worcester is believed to have doubled in the century after 1550 thanks to its thriving leather and clothing trades, making Worcester the largest town in the West Midlands.

The Tything population would have included some people who hoped eventually to enter the city, but were prevented for a time by guild restrictions from carrying on their trade there. Others though, undoubtedly wished to keep well out of the way of the city authorities. Court records of the time show prosecutions of defendants from the Tything - those that is who could be got to court - for brothel keeping, theft and "keeping a dog which hath oftimes bit divers people". Alehouses, most of which were unlicensed and therefore unregulated, gave rise to a number of prosecutions for selling short measures, allowing "diceing tables and unlawful games" and harbouring thieves.

Only the county sheriff had jurisdiction in the Tything and he had a hard time maintaining his authority. In 1633, while trying to arrest one Thomas Cooke, the sheriff's bailiff was set upon in the Tything by six of the inhabitants, three of them women. In the confusion Cooke made good his escape. It was not only the feckless who were lawless; between 1629 and 1637 seven householders from the Tything and the wife of one of them appeared before the county quarter sessions while a further six stood surety for others. John Asbie was one such property holder continually in trouble for sub-letting to people the authorities regarded as

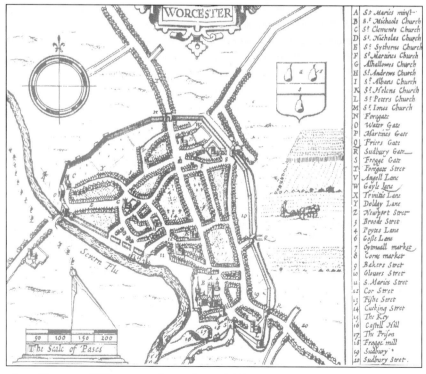

Speed's map of Worcester, from about 1610, showing northward expansion

30.

undesirables. In 1637 he was brought to court, again, accused of housing "a lewd woman, allowing divers lewd persons to keep her company in the night time and so permitting her to be unlawfully begotten with child upon his own bed".

It is ironic that this unholy community was on church land, much of it owned by St Oswald's. This is even more ironic when you consider that, though it might be unlikely they would want to, inhabitants could not readily seek salvation since they, like the people of Barbourne at that time, had no church. When they did attend church, which, wrote one contemporary observer, was "very seldome god knowes", it would usually be St Nicholas in the city, but they had no rights to christening or burial there, being parishioners of Claines two miles away. Church attendance in those days was not the voluntary activity it is today, and Tything inhabitants were 'presented to' both civil and ecclesiastical courts for non-attendance, but with about as much success as was ever experienced in trying to enforce the law thereabouts.

The matter much vexed prominent Oxford cleric Samuel Fell, who became master of St Oswald's in 1631, and he decided that the only solution was to rebuild the hospital chapel, which many in the area had come to regard as their 'parish church'. It was completed seven years later, but history does not record whether the event prompted any upsurge in church attendance.

During this period Barbourne was probably protected from urban expansion by the tenants of Whitestones manor, who would not have wanted an evil-

The chapel built at St Oswald's after the civil war. It was replaced by the present building in the 1870s. Courtesy of the Venerable Frank Bentley, Chaplain of St Oswald's.

smelling urban sprawl surrounding them, and the northward thrust of the city was still halted at St Oswald's, but the city was tentatively reaching out to the pleasant green fields beyond the Tything.

In 1558 the prominent city clothier Thomas Wylde, whose family is recalled by Wylds Lane, gave much of the land comprising Pitchcroft to the city on condition that it established a free school within two years of his death. The area was then known as Pichecroft, having acquired its name from a Norman family called Pyche after the Conquest, and it was split into two unequal parts. Wylde gave the whole of Little Pitchcroft, roughly the area where the south end of the racecourse is now situated, to the city and four and a half acres of Great Pitchcroft, and thus Worcester's great recreation area came into being.

The Civil War

The first northern expansion of the city was abruptly halted in the mid seventeenth century when Worcester stood out for the king and most, if not all, of its first northern suburb was destroyed, mostly by the city to deny cover to attackers. The slums of the Tything were either pulled down or burnt and many poor people from that district were dispossessed.

How Barbourne fared in this period is not recorded, but the war must have brought disruption and distress to the lives of the people here as it did to many others, and no doubt at times they fled in the face of an advancing army only to return and find their homes and crops despoiled, their livestock taken and their livelihood destroyed. Worcester was twice involved in major engagements and the remaining monastic buildings at the convent and the hospital would have made useful billets; 500 men were at one time said to have been quartered at Whiteladies and later excavations were said to have discovered skeletons there of the civil war period.

As in later centuries, Pitchcroft proved a useful marshalling ground for the military of both sides. According to one story, Charles I's dashing young cavalry commander Prince Rupert almost came to grief there while in the city. After a good breakfast he went out to Pitchcroft with some fellow officers and became so engrossed in firing at effigies of parliamentary leaders that he failed to notice a troop of 500 parliamentary horse until they were almost upon him. The royalists quickly retired into the city in some confusion.

Before the second battle of Worcester, on 3 September 1651, the future Charles II planned to assemble a major force on Pitchcroft recruited from the local population, and he called on all men in the county between the ages of 16 and 60 to attend on him there. But locals had no liking for the Scots forming the bulk of the future king's army, whose savage conduct earlier in the war was still remembered, and when Charles arrived at Pitchcroft he found that hardly anyone had turned out to support him.

He was susequently defeated and, fleeing from the battle, was said to have paused at Barbourne Bridge to take stock of his situation. According to a later account, Charles wanted to head for London, there to take ship for France before news of his defeat arrived, but his officers counselled that this was too dangerous and he was persuaded instead to slip away from the northward-fleeing remnants of his army and take the Ombersley Road towards Stourbridge.

Thus his famous exploits over the following six weeks, hiding in a Boscobel oak with his pursuers searching below, and finally making good his escape from England disguised as a manservant - the adventures which he never tired of retelling throughout the rest of his life - were the result of a decision made at Barbourne Bridge.

PART TWO
THE GROWTH OF MODERN BARBOURNE

The Rebirth of the Northern Suburb

When rebuilding of Worcester's northern suburb began after the restoration of the monarchy in 1660, it was to become a very different suburb, with fine houses for the wealthy. Worcester's expansion was eventually to continue on into the age of the 'common man', with the first decent housing for working families, but this very different late seventeenth century development marked the second northward expansion of the city and the start of modern north Worcester.

Before the wealthy had a chance to begin colonising the area however, some of the previous inhabitants, with nowhere else to go, returned and built cottages which survived for a time amongst the grand houses.

Two cottages, which apparently served as shops, survived until the late nineteenth century on the site of 59 The Tything. It may be another small row of cottages, albeit with a later 'fashionable' brick front added in the eighteenth century, which survives on the corner of Little London today; if so, then they are the only remaining link we have with the rebirth of the northern suburb and these are undoubtedly the oldest buildings in Barbourne.

These old cottages on the corner of Little London might originally have been built after the civil war, and if so, could be the oldest buildings in the area

The county justices had tried to rid the area of Foregate Street and The Tything of the poor in 1635 before the Civil War, and in 1662, after the restoration of Charles II, they decreed that all tenants not contributing to poor rates must leave the area, leaving the way clear for the middle classes to move there in their place.

The establishment of a 'poor house' in Foregate Street in 1702 also helped to remove the poor from other sites in the vicinity. This was not simply a question of hostility to unsavoury neighbours; it was a matter of avoiding the dreaded 'poor rate', levied to support those unfortunate citizens who could not support themselves.

Avoidance of the poor rate was often a pressing reason for solid citizens to move out of the city and that was as true of removal to the Tything as it was to Sidbury, which was on church land and thus outside city jurisdiction. If you couldn't avoid the poor rate, then at least get it shared out as widely as possible. In 1693 the parishioners of Claines successfully petitioned to avoid supporting the poor of the Tything, claiming it was an independent township of old, and thus they had the responsibility passed to the hundred so that their personal liability would be much decreased, even though the Tything was indisputably part of Claines parish at that time.

Hearth tax for Foregate Street shows that many of the houses boasted five or more hearths and were occupied by gentlemen using the title Esq. Dr John Wall, of Malvern water and Worcester Porcelain fame, is said to have built himself a house in the area which was situated in front of the Green Dragon Inn, and a pleasant walk from the Tything down to Love's Grove and on towards the river may have been on land he held, since it was known as Dr Wall's walk.

The virtues of the area were, according to local historian Valentine Green, featured in an advertisement in a local paper which described the area as having the advantage of being in the country whilst being in the middle of the town. It had also, said the ad, been described as a place to retire to without "absolutely taking leave of society". In 1662 it was complained that "mucke" was being dumped on the highway between Barbourne Bridge and the city boundary, which sounds fairly rural.

The Worcester City boundary lay at the corner of Salt Lane, renamed Castle Street in 1813 after the building of the County Gaol there, and beyond that point the area fell under the authority of Droitwich. The people who lived in this area paid poor rates to Droitwich and had to travel there to register births, deaths and marriages. It was not until 1837 that Barbourne Brook was declared the northern boundary of the City of Worcester by an Act of Incorporation, and remained so for half a century. Barbourne at this period still very much retained its rural character, but change was on the way.

In the eighteenth century Barbourne had become the mecca of the city's wealthy and a string of mansions with substantial grounds spread out along the Barbourne Road, turning the rich meadows of the Ludadingas and their descendants into 'Millionaire's Row'. The building of grand houses in Barbourne Terrace, for example, can be dated at least to 1759 from the earliest deed to a property there in the county archives.

Diversions sprang up north of the city for the benefit of fashionable society, the most notable of which were at the Saracens Head Pleasure Grounds. The pub, which still stands at the head of The Tything, then had substantial lands attached. The pleasure gardens included a bowling green which was a favourite with the most exclusive members of society, and next to the green was a patch of land which was used for travelling performances such as circuses and preachers.

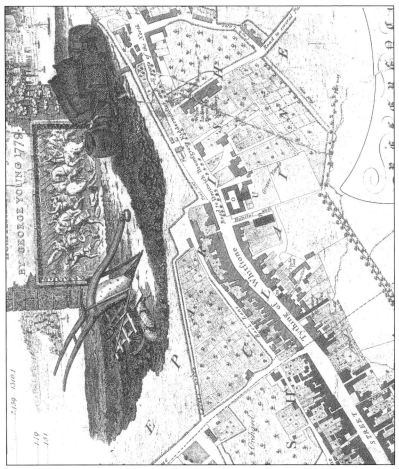

Barbourne 1779 - a patchwork of fields with the occasional mansion

One preacher was said to have drawn a crowd of at least two thousand people. The gardens also hosted boxing matches and even hot air balloon events in the mid nineteenth century.

On 7 January 1824 Barbourne must have been swamped, as was the rest of the city, by visitors flooding in to attend probably the most famous single event ever to be held on Pitchcroft. Tom Spring and Jack Langan were respectively English and Irish bare-knuckle champions, who were fighting for the Championship of All England, and 30,000 people came from all over England and Ireland to watch.

On the day, every inn was full to bursting and Berrow's Journal noted that "the yards of all the different extensive inns were not sufficient to contain one half the carriages". Two temporary stands for spectators collapsed, one before the fight even began, either killing several people and injuring hundreds or injuring 16, depending which account you believe. Spring finally took the title after two and a half bloody, bruising hours and local innkeepers no doubt made even more than the 300 sovereigns (£315) each that the two boxers pocketed.

One perhaps less desirable attraction nearby was the public gallows near Salt Lane (now Castle Street), on which malefactors were despatched into the hereafter before large crowds.

The Berrow's Journal of March 1805 recorded one Henry Young being publicly executed there for attempting to defraud Worcester glovers Knapp & Lea with a false bill of exchange. The report records that he sang hymns on the scaffold and some nearby onlookers joined in.

In 1816 John Batty was hung for stealing a quantity of seven shilling pieces, a bank post bill and several articles of clothing. Callers at the County Gaol in Salt Lane could have the condemned paraded for their curiosity, in return for a small

The Saracen's Head Pleasure Grounds, fashionable in the eighteenth and nineteenth centuries. Courtesy of Worcester City Museums and Art Gallery.

fee to the gaoler. Public whippings, often for quite minor offences, were also popular with the crowds.

Hangings were not that frequent but Worcester had its share, if not more. Between 1868, when public executions ended, and the end of the century, Worcester had seven hangings, which was one more than Birmingham in the same period and four more than Hereford.

Despite its veneer of urban development, Barbourne essentially changed little. If you could look beyond the grand houses and their grounds, Barbourne was still substantially rural. A plan detailing some of the land ownership in the area in 1808 shows a cow pasture beside St Oswald's and substantial onion growing near Barbourne Brook and this pattern of ribbon development combined with traditional rural activity continued well into the nineteenth century.

One aspect of Barbourne which was not improved in this period was the main road, which declined after the salt trade was diverted from Worcester and became a mere gravel way churned up by carriages and horses until it was in a dreadful state of repair. This must have been galling for the inhabitants since the main road had been taken over by a Turnpike Trust in 1714 and they had to pay to drive or ride out of Barbourne.

By the late eighteenth century there was a well-established suburb stretching out of the city to the north. Directory listings for 1790 show Foregate Street contained an eclectic mix of attorneys, glovers, hairdressers, physicians and surgeons plus a horse dealer, a corn factor and a couple of tailors, amongst others.

The Tything had more attorneys, glovers and tailors, together with a butcher, a banker, a builder, a baker, a fruiterer, a gardener, a hairdresser, a tea dealer, a stay maker, a hop dealer, a livery stable keeper and three inns. However it also boasted the homes of a good many of the city's well-off, including William Thomas, the Under-sheriff for Worcester.

Barbourne had become a fashionable hamlet outside the city and needed a fashionable High Street, which it acquired with the building of an elegant terrace named Paradise Row beside Little London, though ironically this was then in the Tything. Now the professional and middle classes could also enjoy the advantages of country living just outside the city, which were previously the sole preserve of the rich, and the race was on to develop more housing in the area.

The Birth of Modern Barbourne

The housing development at Britannia Square, the base from which Roman Barbourne was probably administered, was mooted in 1818 and begun just two years later. Today it is described as one of the first, if not the first, planned housing developments for the city of Worcester, but ironically, at that date it was actually outside the city. It was also - just - outside Barbourne, but the development of this area marked the start of the growth of Barbourne as we know it.

It was not a planned housing development in the sense that we would understand it today; as a development conceived and built by one builder or developer. The land owner divided the area into plots for housing, but these were then purchased by an owner or developer for building. There was no such thing in 1820 as a developer able to build an estate or a bank prepared to support such a venture; the first such built development in the area was at York Place in the 1830s, and it was financed by a society of individual investors.

Prior to the start of the Britannia Square housing development the land was growing flax, used in making linen. Within a decade of the start of building the square was completed as we know it now, and St George's Square went up about the same time. Now the shopkeepers and merchants could also breathe the country air enjoyed by the professional classes and the really wealthy. The fine houses of Barbourne also housed a number of boarding schools, providing education mainly for young ladies who would have come largely from outide the area, and some properties were in multiple occupation from an early stage, suggesting even the well-off were sometimes hard-pressed to take more than a suite of rooms in these grand houses.

The lower middle classes, the clerks and skilled workers, were still excluded from this sylvan paradise - but not for long. In the 1830s a scheme begun by a local businessman and a wealthy investor from Shropshire built around 60 small terraced houses at York Place, just north of Britannia Square - the first known built housing development in Worcester - and the age of the common man and woman arrived in Barbourne, or rather returned since Barbourne began its recorded history as the home of a hard working Anglo-Saxon family.

Despite these important developments, and a distinctive character over many centuries, Barbourne had no separate 'official' identity. A map of 1835 shows the parish of Claines sweeping across Barbourne and almost into the heart of the city. The parish, which was established in 1218, still included the whole of the Tything and Barbourne, Sansome Fields and as far south as Lowesmoor; in fact everything outside the line of the medieval city walls, north of Castle Street and west of Lowesmoor Wharf, was part of a parish whose heart was two miles away. Parishioners had to trek there for weddings, christenings and burials, though St Oswald's chapel continued to serve the functions of a parish church for regular service, as it had for centuries past.

Barbourne, as ever down the centuries, was in need of a church of its own and to supply this need one was built in St George's Square by 1830 at a cost of £3,500, £500 of the money being put up by Sir Henry Wakeman of Perdiswell Hall and the rest by subscription.

It was a church which came to mean a great deal to its congregation but it was

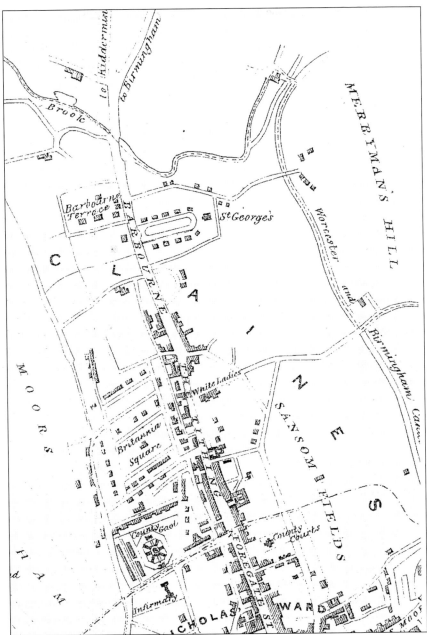

North Worcester in December 1835, showing the parish of Claines sweeping across Barbourne and The Tything, almost into the heart of Worcester

not what was required by the wealthy and fashionable community surrounding it. It was a large, plain, unremarkable building - journalist and historian John Noake, writing in 1868, called the architecture "poverty stricken" - and worse still, it was not a church in its own right, but a chapel of ease to the parish church at Claines.

It did however bring to the area Rev James Tyrwhitt, the first curate of St George's, who started the first school for local children in a cowshed on a vacant plot in St George's Square.

Not everyone was scathing about the new building; the Berrow's Worcester Journal of 28 October, 1830, said: "The edifice has a very neat appearance from the Birmingham road and the interior is fitted up and ornamented in excellent taste". The major problem was that it was simply not big enough and that was to be its ultimate downfall.

St George's chapel, opened 1830, closed 1893. Pictured in 1888 in the parish magazine.

In 1832 a report was presented to parliament outlining the situation with regard to Worcester's burgeoning suburbs and proposing completely new boundaries for the city.

At that time the city's boundaries were exactly as they had been in medieval times, but the population was not. In 1680 there were around 9,000 citizens of Worcester, which was probably not much different from the population at the time of the Conquest. By 1821 there were three times that number and the population had doubled in the previous twenty years.

The coming of the canals may have been a major factor in this growth; in 1772 Worcester was directly connected to Birmingham by both the Birmingham and the Staffs & Worcs canals. In all directions suburbs were spreading fast. "To the northward (the town limits) exclude a great portion of the main streets of the town together with an extensive suburb," said the report, and it added, "both within and beyond the boundary of the Tything, the building of streets and rows of dwelling houses, as well as of detached residences of a very superior class, is going on rapidly".

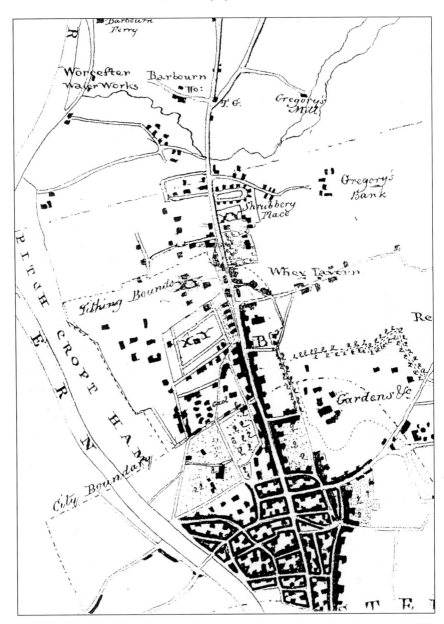

A map of about 1830, showing the city boundary prior to the changes of 1837 and the bounds of the old Tything township. At this date much of the land in Barbourne, and around the Tything, was still in agricultural use

The city had good reason to bemoan the exclusion of many residents from within its boundaries. The report pointed out that there were 909 properties in Worcester as it stood which were assessed for Inhabited House Duty, but it estimated that there were up to 800 properties eligible for duty in the areas which would be brought into proposed new boundaries; which would almost double the duty due to the council overnight.

Better yet, as the report pointed out, "the proposed boundary has been made to include a very considerable area which at present consists of gardens, or pastures and meadows (but which) will, in the process of time, gradually be filled up by villa residences, streets and rows of dwelling houses, as well as of detached residences of a very superior class". You can almost hear the council finance officer rubbing his hands in glee!

A parliamentary commission was set up to advise on the Worcester boundary and wards but it took five years for their report to appear; the commissioners complained that the work had been very difficult because "the manner in which rates were determined made it practically impossible to determine the value of some wards". The method of rate calculation to which the commissioners alluded was apparently known as "scowl of brow".

A Bill was introduced in parliament, based on the report, and on 15 June 1837 Berrow's Worcester Journal made some mild administrative criticisms of it, but not a single letter or article appeared in the paper in the months that followed, either for or against the proposals; if there was any public debate about the move, it was not going on in the local press. Most likely, the Act was seen as simply giving administrative credibility to the de facto reality; Worcester had spread beyond its boundaries and those boundaries were now about to catch up.

On 1 November 1837 the city boundary advanced at the stroke of a pen across Foregate Street, The Tything and out to Barbourne Brook and the inhabitants of Barbourne and the Tything, who had been independent for more than 900 years, and had formerly given their address as 'near Worcester', woke up to find themselves residents of the city. But Barbourne's independence was not to be so easily forfeited.

In 1862 Barbourne, which had retained its own distinctive character and identity for centuries past, was finally awarded the 'official' status of a parish, albeit an ecclesiastical rather than a civil parish, when the church of St Stephen was built in Droitwich Road, taking as its parish the area formerly known as South Claines and now comprising much of the city north of Barbourne Brook.

Ironically the church might actually be outside Barbourne, depending where you think Barbourne ends - the area in which it stands was then referred to as North Barbourne - but nonetheless it was the first church to bear the name of Barbourne. The church was built thanks to the generosity of a local lady, Miss Jane Lavender and her sister Mrs Mary Gutch, and still thrives today.

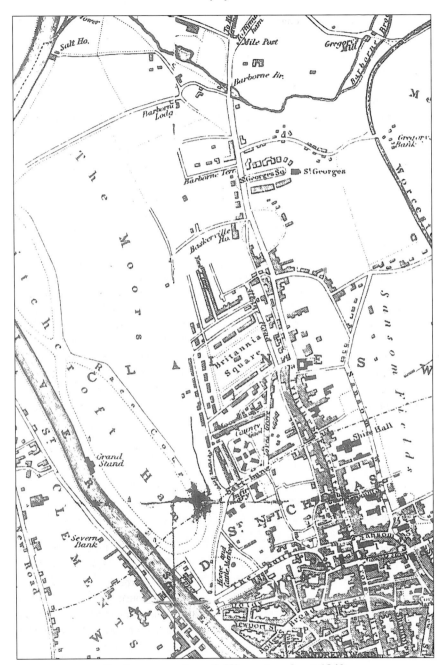

Barbourne and north Worcester about 1840.

In that same year the chapel at St George's Square was given its own parish, stretching from around Little London to Barbourne Brook, and was accorded the right to its own registers. Work subsequently began on St Stephen's School on land also donated by Miss Lavender and Mrs Gutch and it opened in 1864.

Around this period the modern suburb was beginning to take shape but it remains an elusive, shadowy shape to historians. On 21 July 1866 The Builder magazine, which kept architects and builders abreast of current events, noted that in Barbourne "within the last year or two a little town has sprung up", but this tantalizing glimpse of the growth of the area was the only mention the magazine made of the development of Barbourne throughout the half-century from 1843 to 1890 in which the modern suburb largely developed.

Two years earlier, in a letter to that same magazine, Worcester Herald sub-editor and local historian John Noake noted that development of massive railway workshops and of the city's many trades, including vinegar making, Worcestershire sauce, gloving, china, coach building, engine works and more, had quickly increased the city's population by more than 5,000 to around 35,000, and led to "immense blocks of buildings, like little towns", in Sansome Walk, Chesnut Walk, the Blockhouse, Happy Land, London Road, the Moors and Barbourne, which "have so transformed the place that you would scarcely recognise it now" - but infuriatingly, he gives us none of the detail about where, when and how, which we so desperately want.

Despite this lack of detail there is no doubt that the area was growing apace. In 1873 Barbourne was described as a "thickly populated suburb of the city", and 20 or more new streets appeared in a directory of that year, though directories have their drawbacks as sources of information. Street directories, which were a sort of Victorian equivalent of the telephone book, though with additional information, listing names, addresses and often also occupations of residents, street by street, did not generally begin to appear in Worcestershire until the 1870s, and reliable ones not until the 1880s.

In this respect Mancunian directory publisher Joseph Bentley was ahead of his time. His directory of Worcestershire was dated 1840 though printing, which was done in Birmingham, was not completed until 1843, and it included a street directory of Worcester for 1841-2.

The street pattern at this date was very different from that of today. The main north-bound thoroughfare followed much the same route as today, though it was then simply Barbourne, the 'Road' not being added until the 1890s, and Lansdowne Road, formerly known as 'Cut-Throat Lane', cut across what would become the grammar school site to connect with what is now the Upper Tything, south of Little London. Beyond that there were few of the streets we are familiar with.

There were only eight street listings in Bentley's directory for the Barbourne area. They were:

Albany Terrace	Barbourne (Road)
Barbourne Terrace	Britannia Square
Britannia Place	Chestnut Walk
St George's Square	York Place

Whilst we must applaud Mr Bentley's enterprise in producing a street directory at this early date we have to point out that it has its shortcomings. There is no mention of St George's Lane North, for example, though the school of that name had opened there in 1835 and the lane had been shown on a map about five years earlier. It has to be said though, that he was not the only one to ignore the lane; it was first mentioned in a guidebook, minus the 'North', around 1851 but did not appear in a street directory until 1874, and not with the 'North' added until 1880.

The problem for directory publishers was that few, if any, of these new thoroughfares had been simply carved out of the fields which had preceded urban development; most had been in use as tracks or lanes for generations past. By 1830 many local roads were recognizable on maps including Lansdowne Road, Little London, Tennis Walk, Thorneloe Walk, Sharman Street, Barbourne Lane, Pitchcroft Lane, Waterworks Road and Lavender Road, but it would be some time before any were named.

An anonymous writer in the Worcester Herald of the late 1920s was able to give a first-hand account of some local lanes in the 1850s. He recalled that Sansome and Chesnut Walks were then still mere footways and in spring the latter was "a vision of chesnuts, hawthorns and 'golden chain'", but the advent of wheeled traffic made them cart tracks "and bad ones at that".

A map of 1859 shows some housing between the Droitwich and Ombersley Roads, probably farm or nursery cottages, where Union Place, Vine Street, Pinkett Street and Seymour Avenue are now situated, but these streets were not named, they were simply lanes or tracks at that date, though later housing development closely followed the line of these tracks which were then turned into the streets we know today. A rare exception is Park Avenue, shown on a map of the early 1880s as a proposed road carved out of fields to the west of Ombersley Road, apparently intended to give access to a proposed church at the junction of Park View Terrace and Tower Road. The church was never built there, but the avenue went ahead anyway.

Many of the first records of streets betray their origins as former lanes and tracks. Alma Street was first listed in a street directory as Alma Lane in 1873, not being named as 'Street' until 1884. It also included a terrace of houses called Summer Place which later became Summer Street. Crown Street also first

appeared in a directory in 1884 but it had appeared as Crown Lane four years earlier. Checketts Lane was a rare example of a name going against the trend, first
appearing as Checketts Street in 1884 and not reverting to its present name until
1896.

After Bentley's directory the next publication to list streets in the area was
Percy, Butcher & Co's street directory of Worcester, but it did not appear until 30
years later and it included many additional addresses in and around Barbourne.
Some, such as St George's Lane (still without the 'North'), had clearly been in
existence for many years earlier, and York Place was somehow omitted, but
undoubtedly others had sprung up in the development of the 1860s. They included:

Alma Street	Back Walk
Barbourne Lane	Britannia Road
Chestnut Row, St, Place	Cumberland Street
Droitwich Road	Lansdowne Street
Little London	Melbourne Terrace
Mill Lane	New Bank Street
Northwick Lane	Northwick Terrace
Ombersley Road	Sandys Road
St George's Lane	St Oswald's Road
St Stephen's Place	Summer Place
Thorneloe Road	White Ladies Close

This evidence of street development certainly suggests considerable growth in
Barbourne in the 1860s, in line with John Noake's comments in The Builder,
though there is no information at that date on what exactly was being built and
where. Planning application records do not begin until 1865 and those for the
second half of the 1860s suggests that developments in this period were not like
the planned housing schemes of the 1820s and 30s but were relatively small-scale
piecemeal developments by individual developers or builders, and thus streets
were often not built complete, but a few houses at a time. Population statistics
though, clearly show that John Noake wasn't mistaken in his assessment of the
growth of the area.

In the ten years 1841 - 51 just 50 people moved into the Barbourne area,
increasing the population to 1373, but in the following decade almost 600 more
residents moved in, a 42% increase, and during 1861 - 71, when Barbourne was
said to be turning into a small town in its own right, around 1500 people flooded
in, pushing up the population of the area to almost 3,500, a 76% increase in ten
years.

During this period the population of the Tything area also grew, but only very

FROM THE CROSS TO BARBOURNE.

[Commencing at the bottom of the page.]

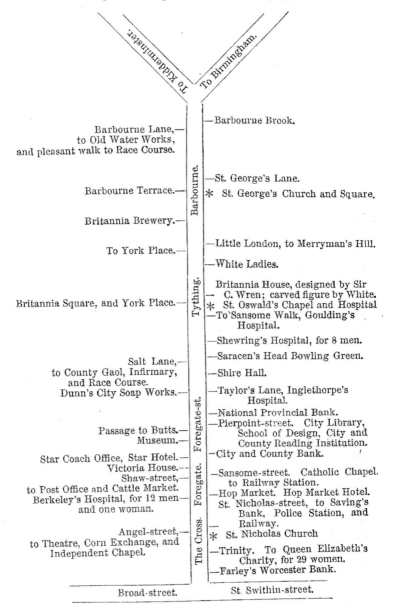

To Kidderminster.

To Birmingham.

Barbourne.

Tything.

Foregate-st.

Foregate.

The Cross.

—Barbourne Brook.

Barbourne Lane,—
to Old Water Works,
and pleasant walk to Race Course.

—St. George's Lane.
✷ St. George's Church and Square.

Barbourne Terrace.—

Britannia Brewery.—

To York Place.—

—Little London, to Merryman's Hill.

—White Ladies.

Britannia Square, and York Place.—

Britannia House, designed by Sir
C. Wren; carved figure by White.
✷ St. Oswald's Chapel and Hospital
—To Sansome Walk, Goulding's
Hospital.

—Shewring's Hospital, for 8 men.

—Saracen's Head Bowling Green.

Salt Lane,—
to County Gaol, Infirmary,
and Race Course.
Dunn's City Soap Works.—

—Shire Hall.

—Taylor's Lane, Inglethorpe's
Hospital.

Passage to Butts.—
Museum.—

—National Provincial Bank.
—Pierpoint-street. City Library,
School of Design, City and
County Reading Institution.
—City and County Bank.

Star Coach Office, Star Hotel.—
Victoria House.—
Shaw-street,—
to Post Office and Cattle Market.
Berkeley's Hospital, for 12 men
and one woman.

—Sansome-street. Catholic Chapel.
to Railway Station.
—Hop Market. Hop Market Hotel.
St. Nicholas-street, to Saving's
Bank, Police Station, and
Railway.
✷ St. Nicholas Church

Angel-street,—
to Theatre, Corn Exchange, and
Independent Chapel.

—Trinity. To Queen Elizabeth's
Charity, for 29 women.
—Farley's Worcester Bank.

Broad-street.

St. Swithin-street.

Landmarks from the city through Barbourne, from an 1851 guide book

48.

slightly, increasing by 149 to around 3000 during 1841 - 51 and by another 193 in the following ten years, a percentage increase of about 5% in each decade, after which it began to slowly decline, though it increased again for a while in the early twentieth century.

The remainder of 'Claines within Worcester', a massive area comprising much of the north of the city as it is today, was also growing, seeing a 26% population increase in the 1860s to 6519, but there was only one other decade in the century in which the growth of this area got above 20%. During the nineteenth century the parish of Claines outgrew every other parish in the Worcester area by a considerable margin, and Barbourne was already outgrowing any other part of the parish - with its major period of growth still to come.

After St George's acquired its own parish in 1862 the Tything was isolated from its mother church at Claines and wealthy residents wanted their own provision. In a bid to keep them within the fold the Rev Smallwood at Claines appointed a curate to the Tything. The area's first dedicated cleric, whose name does not seem to be recorded, did not last long however. Forgetting that a curate's stipend didn't amount to much, the incumbent set himself up at Baskerville House. The rent for this massive property soon landed him in the bankruptcy court and he resigned.

There was now pressure for a separate parish for the Tything. A site for the church was purchased at 28 The Tything and in the meantime services were held in a room at the Saracen's Head.

At this time there were also plans to rebuild the chapel and hospital at St Oswald's, the de facto parish church of the Tything for many centuries past, and a campaign developed for the rebuilding of the chapel on a larger scale to serve both hospital and district. Worcester Herald journalist and local historian John Noake wrote in 1868: "It would not only be a boon to the neighbourhood but I believe it is a right which the inhabitants can demand". But the authorities in London took a different view and subscribers to the parish church building fund grew restive. It was just not to be.

Instead St Oswald's chapel was rebuilt in its present form in 1873 and on 19 March 1875 the Tything became a parish, as yet without a church, though it was civil as well as ecclesiastical, so that many Barbourne addresses were now registered for civil purposes in the Tything of Whitstones, recalling the old tything name which has long since vanished, though it is recalled by Whistone Terrace, a row of late Victorian cottages in Leicester Street.

The Tything site had to be sold to raise building funds and various other sites were looked at, including one at White Ladies, but all came to nothing. Then it was revealed that an anonymous donor, subsequently revealed as the first vicar, Rev Pilkington, had given a site on the corner of Sansome Walk and Northfield Street, originally destined for an off-licence on which building had already been in progress until planning permission was refused.

The new church of the Tything parish would not be in the Tything, indeed it would barely be within its own parish, but a site had at last been found and the large new parish church for the Tything was built in 1876-7 dedicated to St Mary Magdalene, as the chapel of the White Ladies convent had been.

The site for St Mary's, given by the vicar, was valued at £1,300 and the church cost more than £6,000 to build, a massive sum for that time, which was raised by subscription. This gives some idea of the generosity of Miss Lavender and her sister Mrs Gutch in funding St Stephens, though of course the cost of that project was never made public.

St Mary Magdalene was consecrated on 29 November 1877, but unlike St Stephen's it is not still 'in business', having closed on 21 July 1977 and been converted into flats some years ago. Ironically St Oswald's chapel, the Tything's 'parish church' for so many centuries, is still used for worship today for members of the St Oswald's community.

At this period much of the land along Droitwich Road as far as Perdiswell was still owned and worked by the large fruit growing business Barbourne Nurseries, but urban development was gradually spreading beyond the brook and those who could afford it had good reason to get out of Worcester. Many of the city's poor were crammed into insanitary rookeries of slum tenements and courts, and overcrowding and filth brought with them disease and death.

There were regular outbreaks of smallpox, typhoid, scarlet fever and diptheria, and Worcester's recently appointed medical officer, William Strange MD, reported in 1875 that 20% of deaths were of children under five. Death rates were also higher than those in other urban areas of similar size. Worcester was a dangerous place to live and over the course of the nineteenth century the parishes at the heart of the city - St Helen, St Michael, St Nicholas, St Swithin, All Saints and others - all lost population. This was partly because of some slum clearance after 1875, but doubtless it was also caused by the better-off moving out of town.

Suburban development was bringing with it urgent new problems. Barbourne was drinking the same largely untreated river water as the rest of the city - effective filtration wasn't introduced until 1894 - and the primitive sanitation system in the area led to raw sewage being dumped constantly into the water supply. There were frequent serious epidemics of typhoid fever at St Stephen's School and on 21 November 1877 a large number of the area's property owners and occupiers gathered at a meeting at the school to determine what could be done. They decided that the area could not bear the cost of putting things right and there was no alternative but to ask the city to take over.

Not everyone was keen on this idea, seeing the removal of the old turnpike gates opposite the park just a month later as the fall of the last bastion protecting their rural idyll from urban encroachment, but the city nevertheless inexorably spread beyond Barbourne Brook.

Change was slow in coming however. In 1881 there was a particularly severe outbreak of typhoid fever, occasioning much infant mortality in the area, and St Stephen's School, the suspected source of the infection, was closed for six weeks while the crude sanitation system was completely replaced.

At that date the land to the west of Ombersley Road was still an uninterrupted vista of fields running down to the river. Lavender and Northwick Roads were still mere lanes and the only habitation between them was Barbourne Grange and its surrounding buildings, immediately south of the Northwick Road junction.

This was the estate of Mrs Mary Gutch, sister of Miss Jane Lavender and widow of one of the founders of the Farley, Lavender, Owen and Gutch bank on the Cross. She held 71 acres in total and an 1873 register of land ownership gave her estate an annual rental value of £617 10s, which was then a considerable sum and far more than the estates of most Worcestershire land owners were worth.

In her lifetime Mrs Gutch prevented any development between the road and the river, but after her death in about 1880 the land was sold by her executors and soon the city was on the march again and houses quickly spread along the two main roads beyond Barbourne Brook.

Barbourne, looking south from the brook, exact date unknown but probably late nineteenth/early twentieth century. The wall on the right, since demolished, surrounded the grounds of Barbourne College, now Gheluvelt Park. The houses shown are now in use as shops. Courtesy of Ron Shuard.

The 1880s saw some of the most intensive development of the century, both south and north of the brook. Within the St George's chapelry the population almost tripled in this decade, from well under 5,000 to almost 13,000. The 'Claines within Worcester' population, which included the major growth beyond the brook, more than doubled in this period from 7,700 to 15,800. If there was any one decade in which modern Barbourne could be said to have been born it was the 1880s.

In the quarter of a century between 1876 and 1901 there were 457 planning applications to the city council to build more than 1600 homes in Claines parish, most of which are likely to have been in Barbourne. Only three other city parishes saw growth of homes in three figures in the same period; St Peter (627), St John (453) and St Martin (383). Of the 3203 homes planned for the whole city during this period half were in Claines parish and most of those will have been between Little London and Northwick Road. By the 1880s the numbering of properties in Barbourne Road was established essentially as it remains today.

By 1880 Back Lane, Barbourne Walk, Bromsgrove Street, Crown Street, Northwick Road, the shopping parade at Paradise Place and St Stephen's Terrace had all been added to the street directories and also Paradise Row, even though that terrace of Georgian homes had clearly been built in the eighteenth century

Two examples of development on long existing routes were included for the first time in an 1884 street directory; Lavender Road, which made its first appearance at that date, had undoubtedly been in use as an access road or track to Barbourne House and Lavender House since at least the eighteenth century, whilst Waterworks Road was formerly the trackway leading to the water works and the Pope Iron works. Nevertheless the first appearance of these streets in a directory probably marked their first development as residential areas.

By 1885 the directories also included Ivy Street, Old Northwick (Lane), Pinkett Street, Pitchcroft Lane, Raglan Street, Somers Road, Perdiswell Street, St George's Lane South, Tennis Walk and Turrall Street. In that same year the city boundary advanced once more northward, taking in St Stephen's parish and the whole of south Claines parish to create the northern city boundary broadly as it is today.

A further boost to growth came in the 1890s with the development of the Shrubbery estate. The house itself was almost opposite Baskerville House, though standing some way back from the main road. The estate surrounding it was substantial, bounded on the north by St George's Lane South and St George's Church, on the south by Cumberland Street and White Ladies Close, on the west by Barbourne Road and on the east by Flag Meadow Walk.

The estate was still complete at the time of preparation of the first 25" to the mile map of the area in 1884, fringed by pleasant wooded areas and open grass-lands which would not have disgraced many a public park, but within six years

Barboune Road about 1900, with The Talbot in the right foreground and the shops of Paradise Place on the left. Courtesy of Ron Shuard.

the first applications were being lodged for development of the site. It is a sobering thought that if the former Barbourne House estate, which forms the basis of Gheluvelt Park, had come onto the market just a few years earlier, in the late nineteenth rather than the early twentieth century, it too might now be covered with streets of Victorian villas.

By 1896 the massive growth of the area was obvious in the incredible number of new streets appearing in directories:

Berkeley Street	Blanquettes Street
Bourne Street	Brewery Walk
Brook Street	Cypress Street
Flag Meadow Walk	Gregory's Bank
Gregory's Mill Street	Hebb Street
Henry Street	Lyttelton Street
Melbourne Street	Northcote Street
Park Avenue	Park View Terrace
Pope Iron Road	Price Street
Redcliffe Street	Saunders Street
Selborne Road	Sharman Road
Shrubbery Avenue	Somerset Place
St Stephen's Place	Summer Street
Thorneloe Walk	Tower Road
Townsend Street	Victoria Street
Vine Street	Wakeman Street
Woodbine Road	

There does not seem to have been any great increase of industries within Worcester to explain this massive growth; rather there seems to have been a continuing development of all the various trades and industries identified by John Noake in the 1860s, especially engineering. And perhaps more importantly, the development of railways put Worcester very much on the national map and the coming of the trams, or electric cars as they were known in their day, for the first time made mass travel from Barbourne into the city quick, simple and cheap.

Who were the developers and builders who built Barbourne as we know it today? They were not large-scale developers. The story told by the planning application data is of a large number of very small-scale building projects, many of them for single houses.

Not surprisingly, the people applying for developments of more than one property were often in the building trade. On 15 July 1867, builder George Priddy applied for permission to build two cottages in Sandys Road. On 11 March 1872 builder J.H. Beard applied to build two cottages in St George's Lane and builder Charles Higgs applied to build seven cottages in Chesnut Street in October of that year. These were all one-off developments, but some names appeared regularly over a period.

Thomas Insoll, probably a builder though his occupation is not recorded, first applied for planning permission in 1870, for three houses in the Arboretum. In the following 11 years he put in eight requests for planning permission, including five houses and a corner shop in Northfield Street; five houses in Chestnut Street and a further two three years later; four houses in Lower Chestnut Street; two in Barbourne Lane and five in Lansdowne Street.

Builder John Wootton started with an application for two houses in Chestnut Street in January 1875, and put in a further eight applications for 18 homes in and around that area during the next four years. Builder and stonemason John Rouse from Rainbow Hill was also active at that time, applying to build a shop and more than 60 houses over a five-year period, though mostly outside Barbourne. Whether these builders were engaged in property development or, in some cases, were applying for planning permission on behalf of clients is not clear.

The first recognisable property developer active in the area was Edwin Nichols, who must have inherited the high-class furniture

Builder Herbert Ashcroft ensured he would be remembered when he built a complete road and named it after himself. In the background is an oast house which formed part of Spreckley's Brewery, now incorporated into a housing scheme

dealing business he ran, since it was founded in 1800; he submitted his first planning application in August 1877, for two houses in Barbourne Road.

By February of the following year he had formed his company, Worcester Land and Investment, and in the next nine years he submitted at least ten planning applications, mostly for developments in Barbourne, though often they were fairly small-scale, including three houses in "a new street near the Swan Inn", later named Brook Street, and a further two houses in Barbourne Road in 1879.

Nichols hit the property developing jackpot in the early 1880s, after the death of Mrs Mary Gutch, who with her sister Miss Jane Lavender had funded building of St Stephen's Church and school in the 1860s. Nichols was one of her executors and purchased her estate, including all the land between the Barbourne House estate (now Gheluvelt Park) and Northwick, for £2,836. The sale of this land for housing helped fuel the building boom of the 1880s in Barbourne.

Herbert Ashcroft became a developer in his own right, though on a more modest scale, but he began as another of the builders active in submitting planning applications over the years; he applied to build three houses in Lansdowne Road in 1883, four in Nelson Road in 1885, eight in Laslett Street and Lansdowne Road in the following year, four in Lyttleton Street and three in Somers Road in 1887, four more in Laslett Street in 1888 and sixteen in Waterworks Road and Barbourne Walk in that same year.

In 1898 Ashcroft submitted a planning application for 31 cottages in a new road off Hebb Street. Henry Badham, born in Ashcroft Road in 1914, recalls that the road, which first appeared in a street directory in 1905, had been built entirely by Herbert Ashcroft who gave it his name.

The names of J.H. Beard, John Rouse and Herbert Ashcroft continue to crop up in planning records through to the end of the century and, despite Ashcroft Road and some larger planning applications when the Shrubberies estate was developed, Barbourne continued mostly to be built piecemeal, a villa or two here, half a dozen cottages there, by enterprising local businessmen and builders who were prepared to take risks to seize the opportunities open to them in an age of rapid growth in housing demand.

Much of the housing in Barbourne was probably built speculatively for rent. Henry Badham recalls that Ashcroft Road was built for rent and it wasn't until the 1930s, after Herbert Ashcroft died and his son took over, that properties began to be sold off.

In 1888 a three-bedroom house in Waterworks Road could be rented for £1 a month including rates. Some 18 years later rents for four-bedroom houses in Brook Street were £1.50 a month including rates.

At that time a solid Victorian villa, such as 'Linsey House' in Barbourne Road, which had five bedrooms plus servants' quarters, would set you back £25 a year, rates extra.

During the last quarter of the nineteenth century and into the new century Worcester estate agents regularly held sales or auctions of 'investment properties' with existing tenants - many of whom had been in occupation for long periods - and also building plots suitable for small groups of houses, and the majority of these were usually in Barbourne.

Tenants paid a premium for being in the relatively fresh air of Barbourne, as shown by a sale of 'investment properties' by Griffiths & Millington at The Star Hotel, now the Worcester Whitehouse Hotel, in Foregate Street on 27 March 1906, details of which were kindly provided to us by Laurence Harper.

The auction included three terraced four-bedroom houses in Brook Street, now replaced by a housing development, and four four-bedroom 'cottages' in Newdix Court, behind No. 6 High Street, also since swept away by development.

It has to be said that the Barbourne houses had a distinct advantage in accommodation, having an entrance hall, front sitting room and dining room both with marble chimneypieces, kitchen, pantry, small rear yard, use of washhouse and large front gardens, while the 'cottages' off the High Street had only a living room and 'back kitchen with furnace', but despite having the same number of bedrooms, the Barbourne houses had rents of £18 a year which was exactly double

Children playing in Little London in 1903, in a painting by E.A. Phipson. The cottages, known as Talbot Row, were demolished in the 1920s or 30s. Courtesy of Worcester City Museums & Art Gallery.

that of the city centre 'cottages'.

Even so there was apparently no shortage of tenants for properties in both price ranges, since these 'investment properties' were invariably tenanted and often had been for some years.

The outward face of Barbourne was of a suburb of comfortable and even prosperous Victorian family homes, but there was another, seamier side to the area. When the Rev C.H. Pilkington, the first vicar of the Tything parish, arrived in the area in 1875, he and his wife were horrified to find that Sansome Walk, the site of their church, was the habitual haunt of prostitutes. In a rented building in Sansome Fields they set up a Rescue Home which later moved to a house called Melrose in Sansome Walk, subsequently the Diocesan Registry, and finally to a much larger property called Field House in Wylds Lane.

Poverty also had other consequences. In the 1890s a soup kitchen for the poor of St George's parish operated at the Moors Room, a mission in a former racing stable on the edge of the race course. In 1891, during a particularly severe winter, a Christmas Treat and Entertainment was held at the Moors Sunday School, with tea at 6pm and a magic lantern show, followed by distribution of warm clothing. This Moors mission would seem to be the precursor to the Mission Church of the Good Shepherd, run by St George's in Severn Terrace from 1914 to 1938, on a corner site more recently occupied by the Swan Theatre.

Throughout the 1890s issues of the St George's parish magazine repeatedly carried references to the 'St George's District Nurse and Nourishment Fund' and the work of the soup kitchen. As late as December 1920 the vicar, Rev Alan

Poor homes in St George's Lane, painted by E.A. Phipson in 1905. Poverty in Victorian Barbourne led to prostitution and high mortality, amongst the young especially. Courtesy of Worcester City Museums & Art Gallery.

Moutrie Mylne, was writing: "Owing to the short number of boots, a number of our little children in the Infants' School are at present walking with literally nothing between their feet and the pavement. This won't do for the winter. Gifts of little boots (second-hand or new) will be greatly valued".

It was always the young who suffered most; of the 42 people who died in the parish in 1894 a total of 15, more than a third, were aged five or under; in 1896 it was 23 out of 45, or more than half.

In 1894 the area finally acquired a replacement for the 1830 chapel of ease in St George's Square with the opening of a superb new church designed by the finest architect in the land, Sir Aston Webb, at a cost of around £8,000. It was still known as St George's, Claines, however until St Mary Magdalene closed in 1977 and the two parishes were combined.

New developments continued to outstrip the growth of the sewer system. In the early 1890s the county council, anxious to avoid flooding on a main route, raised the height of Droitwich Road, along the centre of which then ran the boundary between Worcester and Droitwich. This caused surface water to run off into Checketts Lane, flooding it so regularly that some local wag advertised the lane as suitable for boating and fishing!

The wrangle between the county council and the two corporations over who should be responsible for remedying this situation went on for almost a decade and it was not until 8 March 1902 that Berrow's Worcester Journal was finally able to report that it had been agreed to provide sewers in the lane.

In the late 1920s it was observed in the weekly Worcester Herald that: "The portions of Claines now absorbed in Worcester must contain at least one-third of the entire population of the city".

Despite Barbourne's growth as a suburb, and its move into the city in the nineteenth century, it has continued to be regarded as 'out of town'. When Hubert Leicester, Worcester historian and five times city mayor, wrote his book *Forgotten Worcester* in 1930 he included a tour starting at "the north end of the city". In fact he started at White Ladies, thus excluding Barbourne entirely!

PART THREE
BUILDINGS AND BUSINESSES

Some Local Buildings and Residents

No account of the residents of Barbourne over the centuries can be anything other than inadequate, since there are so many more human stories than can ever be told, or even known. We have attempted here to take a selection of significant and interesting buildings, past and present, listed south to north, and tell the human stories of their owners and tenants over the years. No doubt there are many more such stories yet to be discovered by other writers in the future.

Britannia House, now the Alice Ottley School, is situated in the Upper Tything and was built for John Somers, a clever and successful lawyer who rose to be Lord Chancellor of England. The architect was once thought to be Christopher Wren, but was in fact Thomas White who built the Guildhall at Worcester.

Britannia House

White trained as a sculptor in Worcester before going to London where he met Christopher Wren who took him to Rome.

In his studies there he prepared sketches and plans of St Peter's which Wren used in the construction of St Paul's, but White turned down a chance to work on the great London church and instead came back to Worcester.

He designed many of the new buildings in Foregate Street and rebuilt St Swithin's, St Nicholas and All Saints churches. Both Britannia House and the Guildhall were built in the 1720s. The figure of Britannia on the front of the house, which gave the building its name, is also said to have given Britannia Square its name. Superstitious Victorians thought the house was haunted after a servant committed suicide there about 1859.

In the 1860's the house became a school for boys and two of the tutors later became well known national figures. Mr Huddlestone was the last Judge of the Court of Exchequer and another tutor, Leycester Lynes, who took holy orders, became well-known, not to say notorious, as a preacher under the name of Father Ignatus, styling himself the first Anglican monk.

In 1883 Britannia House became Worcester High School for Girls, later to be renamed Alice Ottley School in memory of the first headmistress. Earl Beauchamp purchased the house and rented it to the school for a nominal yearly rent. After the Earl's death the school approached various wealthy businessmen to ask for help to buy the property. John Corbett, the Droitwich 'salt king' who built the Chateau Impney, and others came to their aid and the property was secured for the school.

Whiteladies was a farm occupying the site of the former White Ladies convent, now the Royal Grammar School, and incorporating part of the former convent chapel in an eighteenth century building which is today part of the school.

Whiteladies

After the Dissolution the land passed first to John Callowhill, presumably by lease. When Queen Elizabeth I visited Worcester in 1575 she granted it to the city's free school; 'free' meaning free of ties to any particular religion rather than having no fees. The Virgin Queen, coming from the bishop's palace at Hartlebury, passed through Barbourne on Saturday, 13 August 1575, and as a contemporary document says, "did alight at a house neer to the same citie, called Whystons Farme, there to attier herself, in that respect of her wyllyng good mynde to show herself comfortable to the cytyzens". The city fathers turned out in their best satin gowns to greet her at the city liberty post at the end of Castle Street and trade guild members spread themselves along the whole length of the east side of Foregate Street to cheer her entrance to the city.

A black pear tree was said to have been taken from an orchard beside Whiteladies to the Cross during the royal visit and it was supposedly from this tree that Elizabeth plucked three pears and instructed the device be added to the city arms. We are told there are still some black pear trees on the grammar school site today, though they are now extremely rare, probably because it's practically impossible to make anything edible from the fruit.

Though the land had been granted to the free school, that embryonic version of the present grammar school remained at St Swithins until 1868 and the farm in the Tything had a long association with the Somers family; in 1651 the most famous member of the family, and the future builder of Britannia House, was reputedly born there.

John Somers was the son of a Worcester lawyer with land at Severn Stoke but he spent most of his youth at Whiteladies with his aunt Mary who had married brickmaker Richard Blurton, the man credited with constructing the Whiteladies house, which has an eighteenth century front but is probably essentially a seventeenth century building.

Young Somers was himself called to the bar in 1676, quickly making a name as an orator in high-profile cases. He became MP for Worcester in 1689 and in that same year presided over the committee which drew up the 'Declaration of Rights', which is regarded as the basis of our modern democratic system of government. He is also credited with being chief architect of the treaty with Scotland, which turned Britain into the United Kingdom.

Within eight years of entering parliament Somers became Lord Chancellor and was created Baron Somers of Evesham. His career declined under Anne but recovered somewhat under George I. His health was shattered however, and he died in 1716.

He never married and throughout his life, despite building Britannia House, he apparently always regarded Whiteladies as his home and returned there whenever he could. He used his power and wealth to foster his love of art and literature; Swift's Tale of a Tub was dedicated to him and he gave Addison a pension.

In the eighteenth century Whiteladies was home to members of the Blurton and Somers families and the Cookseys of Upton Warren, to whom the lease eventually passed by marriage. Since all three families were related by marriage they lived together at Whiteladies, having their own separate rooms but also using communal rooms for meals and socialising. The Cookseys remained at Whiteladies until the mid-nineteenth century and the buildings they occupied now form part of the grammar school.

Britannia Square, or rather the field on which it was built, was owned by a Mr Handy who lived on the Tything and it was used for the growing of flax to make linen cloth, until northern development of the city made a crop of houses a more profitable proposition.

In 1818 a catalogue and plans for the development of the area were prepared.

The building began around 1820 and is generally supposed to have been completed by 1830, but a map of 1835 shows a number of vacant house plots, though building does seem to have been completed by 1840.

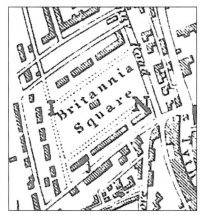

One of the most notable early residents of the square was Worcester's first mayor, Christopher Hebb, who lived at No. 2 in 1842 and later at No. 49. He was a Londoner, born 28 January, 1772, who settled in Worcester around 1793 when he would have been only about 21 years old.

He was a surgeon and apothecary in the days when doctors had to make up the remedies they prescribed and were often judged on their efficacy. His must have worked well for he was highly regarded in his profession and became secretary of the Worcestershire Medical and Surgical Association. He was also an accomplished French speaker and translated into English what was then regarded as the

Britannia Square appears complete by about 1840 when this map was made for Bentley's directory

standard work on heart disease by the French Imperial physician Corvisart.

After city governance was reformed under the Municipal Reform Act of 1835 he was elected as Worcester's first mayor in January 1836 and re-elected in November of that year, unanimously on both occasions. As mayor he presented the city's loyal address to Queen Victoria on her accession in July, 1837.

He founded several charities in the area including one for women which, during the late nineteenth century, was based in the street which bears his name, Hebb Street opposite Little London. When he died in October 1861, aged 89, he left nearly £8,000 to city charities. A full-length portrait of Christopher Hebb, paid for by subscription when he retired as mayor, still hangs in the Guildhall.

Other notable early residents of the square included Harvey Berrow Tymbs, publisher of Berrow's Worcester Journal, at No. 1 and John Rowlands, the original developer of York Place

Christopher Hebb, aged 65 in 1837; a portrait painted on his retirement as mayor. Courtesy of Worcester City Council.

at No. 2, where Christopher Hebb also lived in 1842 along with several other residents including a barrister, a solicitor and an architect. Several of the other houses also had multiple occupants, suggesting that they were rented as rooms or suites of rooms.

There were quite a number of houses which did list single occupants, no doubt with a staff of servants caring for them, but it appears that right from the start there may have been some difficulty in finding enough residents with the budget to match the generous size of these stately villas. Numbers 18 and 19 were lodging houses in 1842 and numbers 8 and 9 housed a ladies' boarding school.

At No. 12 was a police office where the chief constable R.R. Harris and his deputy John Lane were based. No. 11 was acquired by the Catholic church in 1848 and was occupied for some years as accommodation for teachers at the Catholic school and, for about a decade from some time in the 1850s, was itself the site of a school, described initially as a 'Middle Class School for Girls', though it must also have opened its doors to boys since its pupils included not only Lucy and Pollie Elgar but also their brother Edward who took piano lessons there with Miss Pollie Tyler.

Springfield, the large house at the heart of the square, was not begun until 1829 and a map of about that time shows that there had been a proposal to build a chapel on the site, but perhaps commercial considerations took precedence; at any rate, the plan came to nothing.

In 1890 the house was rented by the Worcester High School for Girls, now the Alice Ottley, as a boarding house for 18 boarders. It was run initially by Mrs Vincent, a former governess in Lord Beauchamp's household. In 1904 it was taken over by Mrs Druitt and in 1910 by Miss Tuke, former head of Derby High School. In 1911 the house was purchased by the school and remains part of it still. In 1924 it housed 14 boarders whose families paid fees of 18 guineas (£18.90) a term.

Britannia Square is still regarded as one of the most charming and desirable areas of Worcester and is now a conservation area.

Albany Terrace off Britannia Square, was named for the Duke of York and Albany, after whom York Place was named, and may also have been a project promoted by the original York Place developer, John Rowlands.

It was home in the nineteenth century to H. H. (Henry Harris) Lines who came from a gifted family of artists. He was the eldest son of Samuel Lines, an early-nineteenth century drawing master from Coventry who helped set up the Birmingham School of Art in 1821. Henry had a younger brother who was an exhibitor at the Royal Academy but died tragically young.

Henry Lines was born in 1800 and came to Worcester in 1832. He lived in London Road in the 1840s but moved to 7 Albany Terrace around 1855 and apparently remained in the Terrace until his death at the grand old age of 99, though after some 35 years at No. 7, he seems to have spent the last decade of his life living with his daughter at No. 22. Houses with these numbers still exist in Albany Terrace, but the numbering was completely changed about 1950.

Henry Lines was a landscape painter and draughtsman of great ability and exhibited at the Royal Academy and major regional municipal galleries including Birmingham and Manchester. After his death some of his work was presented to the city by his daughter and still forms part of the Art Gallery collections. It includes about 20 watercolours and line and wash drawings carried out over half a century from the 1830s to the 1880s, depicting ancient buildings in and around Worcester. This collection holds the only surviving visual representations of some now vanished features of the city, including old St Peter's church, the old Deanery kitchens and the Guesten Hall beside the Cathedral.

He also became a keen archaeologist, making studies of the old camps of Worcestershire and the border counties, some of which were published after his death by the Shropshire Archaeological Society.

York Place was the first nineteenth-century housing in Barbourne for working people and, perhaps more importantly, it was the first known built housing development in Worcester. The schemes at Britannia and St George's Squares, which preceeded it, involved the sale of plots to owners who then built their own houses, whereas York Place was planned and built by developers, in the manner we are familiar with today, except that these houses were built to rent not to sell.

The nature of the development was almost certainly due to the business needs of the original promoter of the scheme, Worcester businessman John Rowlands, who lived around the corner in Britannia Square. Rowlands, who is variously described in documents as a timber and a coal merchant, was no doubt prosperous, but not wealthy enough to fund the purchase of the land needed at the rates which would have been demanded for a substantial site near to the fashionable Britannia Square.

These days a developer would take his plan to a bank, but in those days finance was only available by getting the backing of a wealthy landowner.

Doubtless Rowlands was sufficiently astute to figure out that anyone wealthy enough to buy the land would realise that all they then needed was a local agent to sell the plots, and Rowlands could find himself pushed out of his own deal.

If, on the other hand, the plan involved actually building the houses, then Rowlands would continue

The frontage of a typical York Place cottage

65.

to be indispensable as the partner overseeing the progress of building work. He attracted Shropshire landowner Henry Wilding of Hall Stretton, to the scheme as investor but it took four years from planning to the start of building, so they must surely have been working to attract in other investors during that time.

The development was planned on land which was part of the Third Pound Field, presumably one of the areas where livestock for which city tolls had not been paid was impounded, while goods were impounded at the old Pound in Pound Walk, just to the north of York Place. By the 1820s, with the city gates out of use and tolls no longer collected in the same way, the land was available for development.

York Place and the neighbouring Albany Terrace were named for Frederick, Duke of York and Albany. the son of George III, who died in 1827, the year in which the development was planned and a lease was first taken on the land on 21 May. The Duke was said to be a popular and reforming commander-in-chief of the army and there was a Duke of York inn on the Moors before this time, but not everyone was impressed with the Duke's skills as a general and some wag composed in his 'honour' the rhyme:

> The grand old Duke of York,
> He had ten thousand men.
> He marched them up to the top of the hill,
> And he marched them down again.

Construction on York Place was begun in 1831 but in November 1832 Rowlands and Wilding sold out. What happened to Rowlands' ambitious plan is not recorded, but reading between the lines of the dry and dusty legal documents in the county archives it is possible to reconstruct what probably took place.

In most speculative developments the promoter is under pressure to keep building estimates to a minimum to attract investment, but when the builders get to work, and costs start going over budget, the investors can quickly lose confidence and back out, with the result that unpaid builders walk off site, leaving the job unfinished. There is no known record of what happened in York Place but this scenario is the most likely.

The project was taken over in late 1832, for the bargain price of £48, by Worcester skinner, leather seller and glover William Ball, who owned other land nearby, and city investor Harvey Shelton. They may well have hoped to get other city businessmen involved in the scheme, but given its chequered history and the fact that the original investors got badly 'burned', getting investors could have proved difficult and the two businessmen may have found themselves with something of a 'white elephant' on their hands. It is possible that York Place remained only partly finished for something like 18 months.

By late 1833 Ball had moved to Middlesex, perhaps in retirement, and passed his share in the project to his son Philip Ball, a city glove manufacturer, his grand-daughter Charlotte, and distinguished local surgeon, Christopher Hebb of Britannia Square.

Hebb, the founder of a number of local charities, was perhaps more likely to have become involved in the project through philanthropic motives of helping provide decent homes for working people rather than for any commercial gain, but his involvement was the master stroke which saved the project, since he was a leading figure in the local community and someone investors would undoubtedly trust.

The new owners put in £500 each; Christopher Hebb finally got £200 of his money back in 1848, and may also have had the rest at some other time, but there is no record. Together the trio promoted The York Place New Building Society - the 'New' being presumably to distinguish it from any scheme previous owners may have tried to promote - in which members paid £1-10s-0d (£1.50) a month for the construction work and ownership of the houses in the street was decided by way of a vote amongst the members of the society.

Construction of more than 60 houses was largely completed by 1835. Each house had its own 'privy' and each pair of houses shared a well. It may not be obvious when you first enter the street, but the houses are not built in the traditional form of a terraced street; they were mostly built in pairs, making their appearance different and individual but at the same time in keeping with the rest of the street. York Place became part of the Britannia Square Conservation Area in 1982.

York Place always had a fascinating social mix. In 1881 residents included a newspaper sub-editor at No. 1 next door to a newspaper editor, and at No. 4, 12 people squashed into one small house, including cordwainer (boot and shoe maker) John Wigley and his wife and six children and a family of four lodging there.

There were also chemists, glovers, a stonemason's labourer, laundresses, a coachman, a decorator, a plumber, railwaymen, an ostrich feather dyer, a straw hat maker, school masters and mistresses, a printer's compositor from Australia on a visit and at nos. 45 & 46, the little Royal Oak tavern which was a feature of the street until sometime in the 1960s when small local pubs, which were once found in every street, began to disappear. There were also two local shops at various times, both now gone, though there is a ladies' hairdressers.

As late as the 1940s there was a small-holding across the bottom of York Place and allotments surrounded a vehicle access road or track leading into the rear of Spreckley's Brewery until the 1950s when Metal Box redeveloped the site.

In the 1990s a housing development was built across the bottom end of the street, named for a steel-framed windmill which formerly stood on a ridge to the north-east and which seems to have been a product of a Worcester firm, Thomas & Son, which was based at Shrub Hill at the turn of the century but later moved to the Climax Works in Droitwich Road. Mr Thomas senior was kno wnt ol ocal s as 'Pumpy Thomas' and was the great-uncle of popular Worcester musician John Merrick who was employed at the works for a short time as a young man.

Barbourne's High Street

Paradise Row, consisting of a terrace of houses with The Talbot inn on the 'high pavement' at the end of Barbourne nearest the city, was built in the early eighteenth century to form a 'High Street' for the fashionable hamlet of Barbourne, although ironically at that date it was regarded as being in the Tything; it was certainly within the ancient Tything township which extended to roughly where Shrubbery Avenue is now.

In the 1890s trees existed in front of the terrace but they were cut down by the Spreckley brothers who took over the nearby brewery a few years earlier. They also put the mock Tudor half-timbering on the front of The Talbot in the 1920s. Ironically The Talbot does have a fascinating history as a hostelry, which has nothing to do with it being 'olde worlde'.

There was formerly a substantial area of land to the rear of the inn, as there once was to the rear of the Saracen's Head at the top of the Tything. The Talbot meadow behind the pub was a popular nineteenth century venue for 'beast shows' or circuses and it was also so regularly used for political rallies that it was said to be at the heart of Worcester politics for many years.

During the 1832 county elections, which followed the extension of the fran-

The eighteenth century Paradise Row, High Street of fashionable Barbourne

chise in that year, albeit to nothing like the level of today, the Worcester Herald, the leading weekly of the time, was said to 'teem" with references to the Talbot meadow. A later writer in the Herald said: "For a memorable fortnight it was the hub of the Worcestershire wheel".

Since The Talbot was close to Worcester but outside the city limits until 1837 it became a regular venue for meetings of county justices, with sheriffs', coroners' and justices' courts held in a large room to the rear of the building. One of the most infamous cases held there was the inquest on Hemming, the Oddingly murderer who was himself murdered. Concerts were also held at The Talbot in the late nineteenth and early twentieth century.

There were livery stables in the yard at the rear of The Talbot which, in the nineteenth century, were run separately from the inn. In 1884, when the landlord of the inn was Miss Janetta Goode, the stables were run by Joseph William Hughes, who also hired out light carriages and was a horse dealer.

An ad for a horse sale at The Talbot in the Berrow's Worcester Journal of 20 April 1885, offered: "Swap, a beautiful grey, 16 hands high, at Ten sovereigns (£10.50), Thorough-bred Mares at Two sovereigns (£2.10) and a half-bred ditto; and Five Shillings (25p) to the Groom." The inn was said to have: "Good accommodation for Mares and Foals at 9s (45p), Barren Mares 7s (35p) - Corn, if ordered, at market prices".

The Shrubbery was a pleasant estate, complete with attractive walks and gardens, which was situated just off Barbourne Road around what is now Shrubbery Avenue, though it extended as far back as Flag Meadow.

The best known owner of this attractive country retreat close to the city was

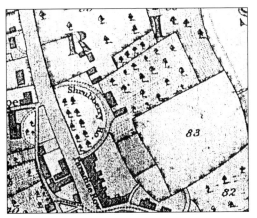

Regency buck Charles Bedford. Bedford was a leading Worcester solicitor with a well-deserved reputation as a 'party animal', but he was also a big man who was always keen to prove his prowess as an amateur boxer and this was to be his undoing.

Incensed at some argument, he picked a fight with well-known local doctor Matthew Pierpoint at Diglis Bowling Green.

Part of the extensive Shrubbery estate in 1884 - a decade before its redevelopment

Pierpoint, who was appointed to Worcester Infirmary in

Shrubbery House in the late 1880s or early 1890s, shortly before the estate was redeveloped. Courtesy of Worcester City Museums and Art Gallery

1819 and gave his name to Pierpoint Street when the city authorities later knocked down his house to create it, was also known to be headstrong - but he was no match for the larger, stronger Bedford.

The fight was regarded by local society as ill-matched and without provocation. Bedford was never forgiven for it and his career never recovered. He died early, having, it was said, drunk himself to death.

The last occupants of the house were the Smith Hanson family, who were city textile merchants. The estate was redeveloped for housing in the 1890s and by 1904 was largely complete as we know it now. Today only the name Shrubbery Avenue reminds us where The Shrubbery stood.

Baskerville House is situated almost opposite Shrubbery Avenue on the end of Brewery Walk and, despite popular conception, it has nothing to do with Conan Doyle's colourful novel of a family haunted by a spectral killer dog. It was built in the eighteenth century by William Smart, a bookseller at 88 High Street and was named after John Baskerville, the renowned Birmingham printer, born at Sion Hill, Wolverley in 1706.

Baskerville was a writing teacher who made a fortune in the 'Japanning' or enamelling business in Birmingham and began experimenting with high quality printing work. Becoming printer to Cambridge University, he produced matchless works for them including some of the most beautiful bibles ever seen, which was somewhat ironic since he was a confirmed atheist who even insisted on being buried in his own garden rather than a churchyard.

John Baskerville

Baskerville gave his name to a new family of fonts he produced which is still in widespread use today, particularly in book printing. One later Worcestershire historian called him "the Caxton of his age".

Smart, a contemporary of Baskerville, was said to be a wealthy man and held the printer in such great esteem that not only did he name his house after him, but on the printer's death in 1775 he is said to have immediately bought Baskerville's remaining stock of books from his widow for £1,100, a very considerable sum in those days.

It would be nice to know more about such a self-effacing and generous man, but sadly no details of his life have come down to us. It is just possible that he may actually have come from Baskerville's home village of Wolverley, since a Thomas Smart, perhaps his father or a brother or cousin, had a mill there in 1746, but there is no definite evidence of a connection. William Smart's bookselling business was last listed in a Worcester trade directory in 1794. In 1842 the house was a ladies' seminary run by a Miss H. Belson. In 1875 it became home for a time to the Rev C. H. Pilkington, the first vicar of the Tything parish, as earlier it had been to the Tything's first cleric, a Claines curate who was almost bankrupted by the expense of such a large property.

By 1889 it was owned by the 'Six Masters' governing body of the Royal Grammar School, Worcester, and in that year it was rented from them by a Mrs Jerram who kept twenty boarders there of the Worcester High School for Girls, later re-named Alice Ottley School.

In 1894 the girls had to move out and a 'new Baskerville' for 27 boarders, named Baskerville Hall, was built in Shrubbery Avenue. Baskerville House was nicknamed Old Baskerville and surprisingly the soubriquet stuck for at least 70 years; it was referred to by that name in the 'Buildings of England' volume for which Worcester was surveyed by Nikolaus Pevsner in the mid-1960s.

After the boarders moved, the house was occupied by Horace Swete MD, the county analyst and a physician who would have had his practice there, but it seems to have remained in the ownership of the Six Masters since it was used as an additional boarding house from 1915 to 1924.

The house was sold by the Six Masters in 1965 and was later said to have been home to the head of the GUS catalogue shopping empire. It is currently split into rented flats.

Thorneloe House, known to most Barbourne residents as the old Eye Hospital, inherited its name from the prominent local family who are thought to have been the first family in residence, in the 1740s or 50s. They did not stay long but may have continued to own land in the area considering the frequency with which their name crops up.

Thorneloe Road and Thorneloe Walk bear their name, as does a sports field beside the northern end of Pitchcroft where Worcester City Football Club started its playing career. There is also Thorneloe Villa opposite Sabrina Terrace and Thorneloe Court in Barbourne Crescent and there was a Thorneloe Lane, still in existence in 1930 but now gone, which was previously called Bedlam Lane and led to a nearby mental institution.

In the 1760s the house, which had tree-lined grounds running back to Thorneloe Road, became a private school, run by a Miss Harris, which continued for thirty years or more; it was certainly still there in 1792. Amongst its first pupils was Sarah Kemble, who was to become famous as an actress under her married name, Sarah Siddons, and has been described by a modern academic as probably the one great tragic actress Britain ever produced.

She came from a touring theatrical family and may have been born in

Worcester. Certainly she made her stage debut here at the age of 12 at a theatre in the yard of the King's Head, opposite the Guildhall in the High Street.

Nineteenth century author Edward Bradley, who was a prolific local history writer under the pen-name Cuthbert Bede, had the good fortune to speak to a centenarian who had been at school with Sarah Kemble and gave a first-hand account of her schooldays.

In those far-off and very different days, being the daughter of players was regarded as being somewhat less than respectable and at first she was looked down on by her fellow pupils, but she won their affection and respect by her cheerful and kindly disposition and, not surprisingly, by her accomplished performances in school entertainments.

Sarah Siddons. Courtesy of Herefordshire Council

By the age of 20 in 1775 she was on stage at Drury Lane, London. Lady Macbeth was amongst her greatest parts and she was painted by Reynolds and Gainsborough and at least three other artists famed in their day, and feted by the greatest figures of her age as the 'Incomparable Siddons'. There is a bust of her in Westminster Abbey.

Around the mid-nineteenth century the house was home to an early Victorian hero, Rear-Admiral Francis Decimus Hastings, who later removed to Barbourne House, living in Barbourne for some 20 years. The Rear-Admiral was something of a man of mystery, perhaps due to a certain modesty very typical of his time and very different from our own, which meant, said a later writer, that "not one Worcester man in a hundred knew he was a hero". But he undoubtedly was, and nineteenth century writers compared his exploits to those of Richard the Lionheart in the Crusades.

He was the hero of the storming of Acre in 1840, which prevented the rebirth of an aggressive Turkish Empire. It was on 3 November that Mehemet Ali, the Turkish Viceroy of Egypt, sought to follow in Napoleon's footsteps and conquer Egypt by storming the port city. His attack was repulsed and on the following day Hastings, who had been wounded in the engagement, was honoured for his part in the victory.

A later resident of the house in the 1860s was Edward Evans who, with William Hill, founded the famous Hill & Evans Vinegar Works in 1830 at St Martins Gate, part of which still survives on Pheasant Street. By 1844, when the business was boosted by the repeal of the duty on vinegar, the premises were already said to be larger than those of the London breweries.

There were eventually 150 fermenting vats and the largest storage vat in Europe, with a capacity of 114,821 gallons. By the end of the century it covered a seven acre site and was not only brewing massive quantities of malt vinegar, but producing a large range of British wines, for export "to tropical and semi-tropical climates", out of raisins, ginger, oranges, currants, cowslips, cherries and gooseberries, as well as quinine wine to combat malaria.

The business remained in the hands of descendants of the founders for much, if not all, of its existence. It was taken over and closed in 1966 and the site is now an industrial estate.

The energetic Mr Evans also helped found the Worcester Chamber of Commerce and, in 1840, the Worcester City and County Bank, one of the earliest joint stock banks, which was originally in Foregate Street. In 1861 a striking new building with classical frontage was built near The Cross, with interior carved work throughout by William Forsyth of The Tything. In 1889 it amalgamated with Lloyds bank though the original name is still visible on the granite facade. Despite all his achievements, Mr Evans does not appear in any of the standard collections of Worcestershire biographies and little seems to be known about him.

When Mr Evans departed from Thorneloe House is not clear. He was presumably the Edward Evans shown in the Victoria County History as having bought an estate at Lower Sapey about 1884, but he must have left prior to that date since a Mrs Reader subsequently ran a large girls' school at the house and by 1884 the Misses Green were in residence, running an academy grandly styled Worcester Ladies' College.

In the early years of the twentieth century it was occupied by surgeon John Paul Cavenagh, who seems likely to have been from Ireland since he obtained his medical qualification there. By 1922 he had been joined by physician and surgeon Bernard Cavenagh, presumably his son.

By 1930 the Thorneloe 'high pavement' was turning into Barbourne's Harley Street, with another practice also at Thorneloe Lodge where physicians Neville Crowe and Stewart Ingles were based. The Lodge still houses a medical practice but Thorneloe House, which was empty for some years after the Eye Hospital closed, was converted into offices in 2002.

Thames House stood opposite St George's Square on the corner of Barbourne Terrace. By its architectural style it seems likely to have been built at some time in the first half of the nineteenth century. Certainly it existed by 1841 when a Mrs Jane Yarnold was living there.

It was subsequently home to the Simpsons who conducted a school there, reputedly the principal private school in Worcester, and a member of the family was said to be a member of the Worcestershire 'Eleven'. In the 1860s it was home to the Rev W. Thorn who had a great interest in studying natural phenomena. He was a popular local eccentric, notable for his loud speech and enthusiastic arm gestures.

By 1884 the house was home to Francis Dingle JP, owner of a warehouse business at Dolday. His chief claim to fame was as one of the city worthies who helped to give Worcester its library and museum.

The new library and museum had been a dream for almost 40 years and Alderman Dingle was amongst the leading figures in the city who formed a committee to make

Francis Dingle

it a reality. The substantial development, fronting on to both Sansome Walk and Foregate Street, also included the School of Art and Technical School. It was opened by the Mayoress, Lady Mary Lygon, on 1 October 1896. Francis Dingle lived at Thames House for more than 30 years.

By 1920 the house was an annexe of Worcester Secondary School for Girls, later to become the girls' grammar school; local historian Ron Shuard reports that the upper sixth girls were then housed there. Later in the 1920s the house was demolished to make way for a new building for the school.

By the 1950s the building was proving too small and a new school was

Thames House. Courtesy of Ron Shuard.

opened in 1962 in Spetchley Road which has since become Worcester Sixth Form College. The school on the Thames House site became Bishop Perowne School, named for a former bishop of Worcester, and it remained so for some years but the site is now an annexe of Worcester College of Technology and Bishop Perowne has moved to the former Samuel Southall School site in Merrimans Hill Road.

St George's Square is said to have taken its name from the dedication of the church which stands at the far end of the square, but there was no church there until about 10 years after the development began. Construction of the square probably began around 1820 and it is possible that it was unnamed at that stage, though considering the leisurely pace at which church authorities tended to take new developments, it is entirely possible that the intended dedication of the church was known at least a decade before it opened its doors to worshippers.

The land on which the square was built was a cow pasture which was divided up into plots and sold off for building, but there were still vacant plots at the end of the decade. The county archives have deeds for properties in the square, presumably drawn up on first sale of houses by the original owners or developers, dating back to 1836.

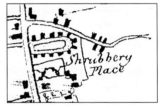

The foundation stone for the original chapel was laid on 11th March, 1829 and the cost of the building (pictured previously), which opened in 1830, came to £3,500, but it was a simple chapel of ease when the wealthy suburb wanted a church, and a grand one at that. The chapel became a bone of contention; people either loved or hated **St George's Square is not named on this map of about 1830. It seems complete but historical sources show there were still unsold plots** its simple architecture and, perhaps most importantly, it was just too small.

Of the house plots still remaining empty at the time the church opened, one roughly in the centre of the south side of the square still contained an open cowshed, and it was there that the first St George's parish school was founded by Rev James Tyrwhitt, the first curate of St George's chapel.

The square had some military connections. On the north side of the square at No. 17, close to the church, was a depot for the Worcester Regiment of Militia. The militia was a sort of local, part-time 'dad's army', which met up now and again to train and was ready to turn out in emergencies.

The militia is first recorded in Worcester in 1799, the year in which Napoleon made himself military dictator of France. The great French military leader had already made teritorial gains in Europe and attacked British trade in the Middle East, and there was considerable alarm in Britain about his continued military ambitions. A volunteer unit was also set up in Kidderminster in that year and others were established in towns up and down the country amid fears that 'Boney' might even try to invade England.

Soon afterwards Berrow's Worcester Journal recorded that: "An English lady of distinction, just returned from France, says she saw, in almost every place she passed, printed bills exciting the French to invade this country, declaring that Britain should be given up to general pillage, and that every man found in arms should be put to death". Men must have 'rallied to the colours" with the same enthusiasm seen when England was in danger of invasion in 1940.

The militia depot must have been the unit's first permanent base. It is not entirely clear why the square was chosen for the depot, since it was outside the city at that time, but there were two possible connections with the area. The militia also had a training ground in the area, Militia Field, adjoining the north end of Pitchcroft, later the first home ground of Worcester City Football Club and now a school sports field.

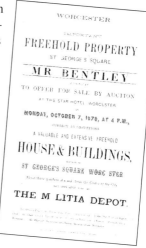

St George's Laundry, probably pictured in the early twentieth century. The building had originally been the Militia depot. Courtesy of Ron Shuard.

In addition, local historian Ron Shuard believes that the colonel of the militia had built a home in the square, at the large white (now white and cream) house on the south side of the church, though there is no sign of him in residence in a street directory listing of 1841-2. If this house was indeed built by the militia colonel, then this property and the militia depot may have been the first two buildings in the square.

The depot was certainly a substantial property, covering 2,275 square yards

including a large house on three floors and an extensive court-yard, enclosed by a "high and massive" brick wall bordering St George's Lane, containing a guard room and two drill sheds, one of wood with a corrugated zinc roof and one of brick meas-uring 81 feet by 18 feet with an armoury of the same size.

It may have had a small per-manent staff; the 1864 Post Office directory lists there Quartermaster Sergeant William De Sour, Paymaster's clerk Joseph Sherwood and Musketry Instructor Sergeant W. Bachelor.

Popular history suggests that the whole square was built to house military officers from the Worcestershire Regiment, but the first street listing of residents in 1841-2, a decade or less after the square was completed, pro-vides no evidence for that. The listing, in Bentley's Directory, included architect Henry Day at No. 12, builder Abel Pointon at No. 24 and a couple of boarding schools at Nos. 16 and 27, but only one man with apparent mil-itary connections, Captain George Timins at No. 10; and whether he was a military man

Several designs were produced for the new St George's Church before this one was accepted. Reproduced courtesy of the church history.

or a sea captain, either active or retired, is not known.

It is likely that army officers were billeted in the square during the first world war, when the Worcestershire Regiment was encamped on Pitchcroft, and that fact - plus the presence of the Militia depot, even though that was a quite separate organisation - may have led to the myth that the square was originally intended for military occupation.

County archives contain a poster summoning Militia members for training as late as 1876 but the Napoleonic invasion fears which had prompted the formation of the Militia had long since faded into history and in 1878 the depot was sold off and became the Barbourne Steam Laundry. A photograph of the premises from

the early 1900s shows a very impressive frontage for a laundry, suggesting that the militia depot facade at least probably remained unaltered.

The laundry closed in the 1980s and flats were later built on the site.

The much-criticised chapel was demolished in 1894, though not everyone was glad to see it go; the church history records that the congregation met there for the last time on 20 August 1893 and that it was a very sad occasion.

A new church was commissioned from probably the greatest architect of the day, Sir Aston Webb, a Londoner who married the daughter of a Dr Everett of Foregate Street.

Webb sounded the death knell for the old church in these words: "..though fairly well-built, it was altogether unsuitable for the purposes of Divine

The design for the chancel of the new St George's Church. Reproduced courtesy of the church history.

worship of to-day".

He was famous for his work nationally and also much admired for his commissions locally. In and around Worcester he designed the Angel Street Congregational School on the corner of The Butts, six almshouses at the Royal Grammar School, restoration work on All Saints Church, Claines Church and St Helen's, as well as the much-praised Memorial Library at Malvern College.

In London his work included a new front for Buckingham Palace, a surround for the Victoria Memorial, Admiralty Arch, Britannia Naval College and the Victoria and Albert Museum.

He planned the front of St George's to echo that of its famous namesake at Windsor, and said after its completion: "The design of the New Church is founded upon that known as decorated, though no archaeological exactness has been attempted, but rather a development of old styles to modern uses and expression".

Lindisfarne House in Barbourne Terrace was commissioned in the late 1850s by the most important Worcester newspaper proprietor of the day.

Thomas Chalk was part-owner of the weekly Worcester Herald which was then the pre-eminent county paper. It was established in 1794 by William Holl with offices at 72 High Street, apparently at the suggestion of Lord Sandys and "other gentlemen" who presumably didn't like any of the existing newspapers in the county, or more likely didn't like their politics.

By 1837 Chalk had become part-owner and for his efforts in keeping it a top-selling Worcestershire weekly he was rumoured to draw a staggering annual salary for that time of £3,000. He spent some of it on commissioning architect Henry Day, who lived nearby in St George's Square, to build him what was considered one of the finest houses in Worcester.

Day also designed Elderslie in London Road and Aldwyn Towers in Malvern, but this Italianate mansion was probably his finest commission. It was originally surrounded by extensive ornamental gardens reminiscent of a fine stately home.

Chalk was a very small man with a very big reputation as an elegant host. City historian Bill Gwilliam described him as "lively and florid, a bon vivant who could tell a good joke". From his desirable residence, Chalk liked nothing better than to drive out in his fine carriage, no doubt enjoying the demonstration of his wealth while raising his hat to acquaintances.

One of Chalk's most lasting decisions was to bring to the Herald, and possibly to Worcester, a man whose contributions to the city, though not always well remembered, outshone those of Chalk himself.

Journalist John Noake, who came originally from Sherborne, became a sub-editor on the Herald, possibly enticed from a job in Birmingham, but he is more familiar to local historians for his prolific notes on local history, published origi-

Lindisfarne House in Barbourne Terrace originally had fine ornamental gardens giving it the appearance of a fine stately home, but these have since been built over. Courtesy of Clive Haynes.

nally in the Herald and later in book form.

Noake's greatest claim to fame however, though it seems to have been entirely forgotten in the intervening years, is as the man who saved Worcester's historic Guildhall. Astonishing as it might now seem to us, in the 1870s there was a move to get rid of the 'old' Guildhall and replace it with a completely new building. Noake was largely instrumental in ensuring that the historic hall was preserved and he was mayor in 1880 when it was restored at a cost of £22,000. Surprisingly, no portrait of him adorns the historic building which he saved for posterity.

John Noake

Chalk's name had disappeared from the Herald by 1869 and his house passed through other hands, acquiring along the way the name that it now bears - in Chalk's day it was called Terrace Villa.

In 1909 it was purchased by George Gascoyne, founder of a city hop and seed business. Mr Gascoyne hailed from Sheffield, where he set up a printing and stationery business, but in 1891 at the age of 26 he brought his young family to Worcester and is thought to have gone to work for Firkins, a hop merchant with a warehouse at South Quay.

Borrowing £1,000 from his wealthy father-in-law he set up on his own and eventually took over seven other local hop merchants, including the one he worked for, and a number of their premises. His South Quay warehouse is now an apartment block known as Gascoyne House, his premises in Little Southfield Street were, until recently, occupied by Lambs, the removal firm, and he also had a four-storey warehouse in Sansome Street, where the Worcester Arts Workshop now stands.

Another of his projects was a partnership to build the Scala cinema in Angel Place and he also owned homes in London and the south of France and had a large tract of land in Canada.

Before moving to Barbourne Terrace, George Gascoyne had built two houses in Park View Terrace in 1895, and for a time the family lived at The Elms while letting off Riverlynne next door. At Lindisfarne the Gascoynes and their four children were much involved in the social life of the area and there are a number of photographs in existence of large gatherings of local societies in the extensive gardens.

In 1911 George was pictured posing proudly in the family car with his only daughter Barbara who lived all her life in Barbourne, having homes in Shrubbery Avenue and later in Sunnyside Road, as well as at Lindisfarne. George Gascoyne died in 1930 aged 64, but his widow lived on at Lindisfarne to the age of 90, dying in 1950. The house was then sold for £4,000 and for some years Dr Crowe had a medical practice there before it became the offices of the National Farmers' Union and Chalk's attractive ornamental gardens were built over. The house is a church centre at the time of writing. The firm George Gascoyne founded was run by his eldest son, also George, until his death in 1953, but it went into decline in the 1960s and closed in 1969. We are indebted to Mr Michael Carter of Droitwich, Mr Gascoyne's grandson, for information on the family.

George Gascoyne with his daughter Barbara at Lindisfarne House in 1911. Courtesy of Clive Haynes.

Barbourne Lodge was thought originally to be a farmhouse, though the evidence for this is not clear. The house and grounds occupied a substantial site at the junction of Barbourne Walk and Pitchcroft Lane, with the house fronting onto the lane and the garden backing onto Somers Road.

It had ceased to be a farmhouse by the early eighteenth century, after which it had a colourful career in various other guises. At the start of the century it was a bedlam or mental institution and a dirt track called Bedlam Lane led to it from Barbourne Road. The name 'bedlam' was a contraction of Bethlehem, the name of the first hospital of that kind in London.

It apparently did not fulfill that role for too long though, since it was referred to not long afterwards as a private residence, having a cockpit used by county teams for cock fighting, a brutal but popular 'sport' of the age.

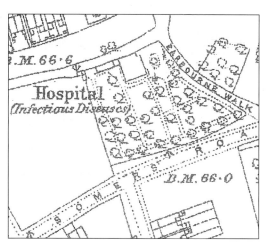

In the 1750s the house was owned, though not necessarily occupied, by colourful businessman John Garway who had a sail cloth manufactory in what is now Gheluvelt Park and was obviously doing well at that time, though in the past he had been declared bankrupt.

Barbourne Lodge shown on a map in 1884, while it was in use as a fever hospital.

The house was occupied from the 1760s by members of the Burney family, relatives of a literary dynasty with links to some of the most distinguished authors and artistic figures of the age, and their arrival must have caused quite a stir in the neighbourhood.

Of the famous Burneys, to which the local Burneys were related, Dr Charles Burney was a prolific and respected writer on music and friend to most of the eminent men of his day including Burke, Garrick, Reynolds and Dr Johnson; his son, also Charles, was a widely-known and much respected classical scholar and his daughter Fanny, the real 'celebrity' of the family, was a leading novelist.

Richard Burney, who came to live in Barbourne with his family of five sons and three daughters, may not have matched the achievements of his famous relatives, but the Burneys were a gifted and well-connected family and it is little wonder that they were prominent in social circles in the city.

Richard conducted a school at the Lodge for dancing and music, both vital accomplishments for the offspring of tradesmen and farmers who wished to be received in 'polite society'. His own offspring christened their new home "Barebones Lodge".

His eldest son Charles Rousseau Burney was a harpsichordist and played at the Three Counties Festival in 1767. He also had his portrait painted by Gainsborough.

Another son, Edward Francis, born in 1760, was a gifted painter and a pupil of Sir Joshua Reynolds, producing some valuable Worcester and Worcestershire paintings, which were published in a collection of "paintings by E.F. & T.F.

Barbourne Lodge, one of the collection of paintings published by Edward Burney in 1784

Burney" dated 1784.

Fanny Burney stayed at the Lodge with her sister, probably before she was famous, and the visit caused some fluttering hearts amongst the young men. Richard's son Charles fell in love with Fanny's sister and later married her whilst Edward fell in love with Fanny, but he was too painfully shy to do anything about it and she later married a French general.

The exact relation between Richard and the more famous Burneys is sadly not clear. It has been suggested that Richard was Dr. Charles Burney's brother but that would have meant that Richard's son Charles had married his own first cousin, which would certainly not have been acceptable, so it is more likely that Richard and Dr. Charles were cousins.

The 1784 collection of Edward's topographical paintings included one of the Lodge which showed a substantial eighteenth century house, clearly not the ancient farmhouse the Lodge had reputedly been, so it was presumably rebuilt at some time during the eighteenth century, either by the Burneys or before their arrival, and the lichen growing on the exterior of the house suggests a date some time before their arrival.

The house was later turned into a fever hospital, a very necessary institution in the days when infectious diseases could cause substantial loss of life in close-ly-packed urban communities, and it was important to isolate sufferers away from urban centres. It was then referred to variously as Barbourne Hospital and the Cottage Hospital.

In 1888 William Strange MD was the physician; by 1892 Mabyn Read MD had taken over. Throughout this period Mrs Esther Coulter was housekeeper and nurse.

A map of 1884 shows tree-lined walks in the gardens of the hospital and it must have been a pleasant environment for those patients well enough to appreciate it.

Improvements in public health in the late nineteenth century, especially effective water filtration in the city from 1894. brought many infectious diseases under control and at the end of the century the hospital moved to Newtown Road, still under Dr. Read's management.

The house in Barbourne was put up for sale but no-one would buy it. This was not suprising considering the awe in which locals held the building, fearing that germs would escape over the high wall and infect them as they passed by.

So eventually the building was set on fire in 1905 by the city fathers to prevent any of the germs which might be left infecting anyone. The fire gutted the interior and the shell of the building was then demolished.

A photograph taken after the fire shows a substantial Georgian building, comparable to that in the Burney painting, suggesting that the house had remained much as it had been in the eighteenth century until its final demolition.

Barbourne Lodge after it was deliberately set on fire to kill any remaining germs lingering from its use as a fever hospital. Courtesy of Worcestershire Archaeological Society.

Lavender House was the home of the Lavender family, who probably built it in the late eighteenth or early nineteenth century on a site just to the north of Barbourne Brook and near the Severn, backing onto a carriage road which is now Lavender Road.

To the west of the house was a courtyard and service buildings and beyond that a kitchen garden. In front of the house was a lawn surrounded by shrubberies. A well was shown just within the western boundary of the property in 1774 but there were also two springs nearby, the water from which probably fed pools within the Barbourne House park.

The Lavenders also held land to the west of Barbourne House down to the river. John Pearkes Lavender, who was in control of the estate by the early 1820s, was keen to develop his land but this led to problems with the neighbours. When he diverted the brook in 1826 several neighbours claimed their land was adversely affected and an inconclusive court case resulted. JP Lavender purchased the Cookes property, including presumably Barbourne House, in 1838 and it has been suggested that the family moved there, but if they did they didn't stay very long since the house had other occupants from the 1850s or 60s.

Around the middle of the nineteenth century a member of the Lavender family was governor of the County Gaol in Castle Street and became involved with someone who, due to the course of events, was nicknamed 'the Worcester spy'. The man who acquired this unfortunate nickname was artist Richard Dighton, who painted respected portraits of many Worcester justices and their officials. Usually his subjects were happy to pose, but Lavender would not agree.

Dighton adopted the tactics used by his contemporary, 'Spy' of the magazine Vanity Fair, in dealing with unwilling subjects. He stalked his 'victim' until Governor Lavender complained to the police, suspecting criminal motives. Dighton's arrest brought him, as he calculated it would, face to face with his accuser and the resultant portrait was accounted by contemporaries a very good likeness.

The family had once had an interest in the Farley, Lavender, Owen and Gutch bank, where the Nat West bank now stands on The Cross. When the bank failed in the 1850s the family were no longer involved, but Miss Jane Lavender was said to be distressed that her late father's signature was on many of the notes issued by the bank, and she reputedly provided funds to honour all the notes with his signature.

Lavender House in 1903 - it was demolished in the 1970s

In 1862 Miss Jane Lavender and her sister Mrs Mary Gutch, wife of another of the founders of the bank at The Cross, gave money for the building of a new parish church, which was to become St Stephen's in the north of Barbourne, and two years later they also funded the building of St Stephen's School. At her death, around 1880, Mrs Gutch owned all the land between the present Gheluvelt Park and Northwick Road, which was then farmland, and the subsequent sale of this land helped fuel the building boom of the 1880s and 90s in north Barbourne.

In 1894 Lavender House was leased by Barbourne College and remained part of the school until it closed in 1908. The house was still shown on a map of 1970 but it was demolished during that decade.

Barbourne House, situated on the north side of what is now Gheluvelt Park and a little way west of the Ombersley Road/Droitwich Road junction, was probably built originally sometime in the early sixteenth century though it is hard to determine an exact date because the documentation which survives is unclear.

Worcester City Council holds deeds for the site but the building on the site is not named, it is just described as 'property', therefore it is impossible to determine if it is Barbourne House or not. What we do know however, is that the house was either built, or perhaps more likely rebuilt, sometime before 1788.

In 1788 the property was occupied by Rev Thomas Cookes. It is thought that this land had been in the Cookes family since the sixteenth century, as there is proof of an estate in Barbourne being passed down through the family since that time.

During the survey of Claines in 1751-3 the Barbourne estate was listed as being in industrial use, with a building over the brook, probably a mill, and part of the site listed as a whitening yard.

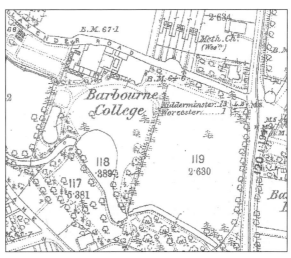

Barbourne House and grounds in 1884, when the house was in use as a school.

The area was leased from Rev Cookes to Mr Garway who was described as a merchant and was using the land for his business.

The house was later leased to Colonel Newport and when he died the auc-

89.

tioning of his well-stocked cellar reportedly caused a minor sensation and the opening of a bottle of 'Newport's port' was said to be the much-anticipated climax to many a special meal in early Victorian homes in the city.

The estate was auctioned at 5 o'clock on 6th November 1837, when it was listed as the 'Barbourne House Estate'. The auction took place at the Star and Garter Hotel in Worcester, now the Worcester Whitehouse Hotel.

The estate was divided into seven lots. Lot one contained Barbourne House along with a coach house, stables, barns, gardens, pleasure grounds and several cottages. The remaining six lots consisted of 'fields' of varying sizes.

It was purchased at auction by JP Lavender of nearby Lavender House and it has been suggested that the Lavender family moved into Barbourne House but if so they cannot have stayed very long since there are reliable accounts of various other occupants. Around mid-century the house was occupied by retired Admiral Hastings, the hero of the storming of Acre in the 1840s, who had lived previously at Thorneloe House. Lavender Road was then a track leading to the house and locals christened it 'Admiral's Walk' owing to the old sailor's habit of pacing up and down it for exercise.

The house was subsequently occupied for some years by the Smith family whose nurseries in St Johns were reputedly the largest in the world at that time, stretching from Bransford Road to Lower Wick. The business was developed in the 1820s by Richard Smith, son of nurseryman Thomas Smith from Lower Wick, and during the following century the nursery passed down to his son and

Barbourne House - Courtesy of Ron Shuard

grandson, both called Richard.

Everything about the business was massive. It covered 157 acres with 18 miles of walkways between rows and displays. It had a 2,300 yard central drive and there were two and a half acres of glasshouses. The nurseries employed 200 people and in just one month, October 1829, sold 10,000 fruit trees.

Smiths introduced the Worcester Permain apple in 1874 and a century later it was still one of the most important commercial varieties in the UK, though sadly it is not one of the limited varieties which supermarkets now sell.

The nurseries gradually contracted as land was sold off and in 1993, more than a century after the family left Barbourne House, the company ceased trading and its remaining land - just three and a half acres - was sold for housing.

In 1881 the estate was sold once more and in 1883 the house became a school, presided over by W.P. Caldwell, and from then on it was known as Barbourne College. The house ceased to be a school in 1908, and during the first world war it was used for a time as a military headquarters.

In 1917 the land was purchased for the city. The city fathers had hoped to put the purchase off until after the war but after pressure from the owner the mayor agreed to purchase the land himself with a view to selling it on to the council when they had the funds available. Barbourne House was subsequently demolished and houses were built for soldiers and sailors who were wounded in the First World War.

Barbourne College grounds, from an 1896 advertisement for the college.

Barbourne Tollgate was said to have been the first in Worcestershire, opened by the Droitwich Turnpike Trust in 1714, initially on a site on Droitwich Road.

Later a Worcester trust was set up and a gate and toll house were erected on the Ombersley Road. The original locations of the gates were shown on a plan drawn about 1751 during a survey of the area. The Droitwich Road gate was a short distance from the fork, but the Ombersley Road gate was much further from the junction, perhaps near where St Stephens School was later situated, probably to avoid travellers ducking down adjacent lanes, not shown on the plan, and avoiding the toll.

It eventually became clear that one joint gate would be a more economical solution for the two trusts and the gates were removed to the junction of the Ombersley and Droitwich Roads, where a new toll house was built. Nineteenth-century Worcestershire antiquarian Dr Peter Prattinton mentioned seeing an advertisement for the erection of the joint toll-house in 1814.

The turnpike companies performed an important public service by keeping the appalling roads of the period in some sort of state of repair and they aimed to recover their costs and make a profit from the tolls they charged. The clearest evidence that they did indeed make a profit is that by 1835 there were twenty-two turnpike trusts in Worcestershire, one for every fourteen miles of road then in existence in the county.

A table of toll charges from that year shows that tolls were then 36d. for a six horse stagecoach and 8d. for a two horse farm cart. The rights to charge tolls were usually publicly auctioned by the trusts or let by tender, generally on an annual basis, though the Worcester trust seems to have let gates for three years at a time.

In 1793 the Droitwich trust let the Barbourne gate for £315, compared to £310 for its Bromsgrove gate and £91 for Hanbury. By 1813 Barbourne was let for £600 compared to £396 for Bromsgrove and £140 for Hanbury.

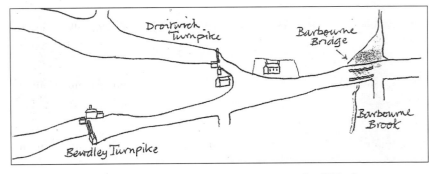

The position of the two turnpike gates in Barbourne in 1751, from a survey carried out by John Doharty Jun. for the Worcester Dean and Chapter

In 1850 the Worcester trust's annual fee for letting of the Barbourne gate was £750 but Powick at that date cost the lessee £2505. By 1866 the annual fee for lease of the Barbourne gate had sunk to £365. It closed, or perhaps we should say opened, for good eleven years later.

The Barban (Barbourne) gate earned national notoriety in the late eighteenth century when the keeper of the gate refused to let the king pass. The monarch in question was George III, who in this case had good reason to be mad.

The King and Queen and their four children were paying a visit to Cheltenham and on Saturday morning, 2 August 1788, they passed through Worcester on their way to visit the Bishop of Worcester at Hartlebury.

They met with nothing but cheering crowds, until that is they reached the Barbourne turnpike gate on Ombersley Road and encountered surly gate keeper Robert Sleath. Robert stopped the substantial royal entourage at the gate and demanded they pay the proper toll before he would let them pass. One of the king's servants assured him that the person who was following His Majesty's entourage would pay the tolls so, on this assurance, Robert opened the gate and they passed, but he received no toll. That was not just a loss to the turnpike trust - often tolls that gate keepers failed to collect could come out of their own pocket.

Robert knew that the king would have to return in the afternoon and when he heard that the entourage was approaching he locked the gate and stood in front of it with the key in his hand, demanding the toll for both journeys before he would let anyone pass.

According to one version of the story the king had to wait for several hours while a courtier was despatched to obtain the funds, which would have been a

George III in 1788 - a portrait painted to commemorate his visit to the city. Courtesy of Worcester City Council.

substantial sum for those days. Eventually Robert was paid by one of the king's men and the monarch was allowed to pass.

If Robert had tried this sort of thing on Henry VIII no doubt his head would quickly have been parted from the rest of him but times had changed and he was never brought to account for his 'defence of Barbourne gate'.

Despite this encounter the royal family returned three days later for a very successful five day royal visit - but they took good care to stay away from Barbourne gate! When Robert died in Birmingham seventeen years later, in 1805, this epitaph appeared in the press:

> On Wednesday last, old Robert Sleath
> Passed through the Turnpike Gate of Death
> To him would Death no toll abate
> Who stopped the King at Wor'ster Gate.

The old joint toll house, built after Robert Sleath's time, is still in existence today, currently used as an antique shop, before that a sweet shop, and remembered by older residents as Mr Cale's paper shop, from which daughter Ethel set out every day to deliver papers, but the old gates were taken down at the end of 1877.

By then north Barbourne was on the verge of being swallowed up by

An engraving of the Barbourne joint toll gate about 1850. The gates were removed at the end of 1877 but the toll house still exists and is now a shop.

94.

Worcester, though the change was met with mixed feelings. Some saw the demolition of the gates as the fall of the last bastion protecting their independence from the encroaching city, as this extract from a poem in the St Stephen's Parish Magazine of February 1878 shows:

> At Barbourne, as in other spots,
> Old Time is still a flying,
> And folks scarce recognise the place,
> Familiar sights are dying.
>
> That barrier of barriers now
> Has yielded to its fate,
> To few a friend, to most a foe
> The stubborn Turnpike Gate.
>
> 'Ere this the envious Pike forbade
> Our free communication,
> But now the Gate no longer stands,
> What stops Amalgamation?

Whether due to the fall of the gates or not, the amalgamation of the area beyond the brook into Worcester went ahead not too long afterwards.

The Water Works

Worcester's first known water works was established just south of the old bridge in the city centre about 1619 and water was pumped into two cisterns from which it was piped into the houses.

The works was rebuilt later in the century at the eastern end of the old bridge. A long narrow islet, whether natural or man made is not known, stretched from the old bridge - superseded at the end of the eighteenth century - to where the present one now stands, dividing the river, and on this islet the water works was said to have been erected.

The narrow channel formed by the islet was called Little Severn and from this the water supply was drawn and pumped into a reservoir at The Cross. The need for a new bridge in the late eighteenth century caused the original water works to be taken down and the islet cleared away to facilitate navigation of the river.

An act of parliament allowing the city to replace its old water works was passed in 1770 and it was supposedly in 1795 that the waterwheel and pumps were removed to Barbourne, though a water works in the area was listed in a directory of 1790 with a John Tyler in charge.

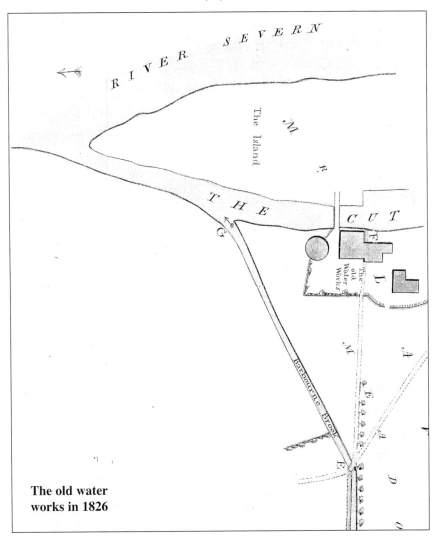

The old water works in 1826

Barbourne brook was diverted away to the south of the site and a 'cut' was dug to divert water from the main river channel. A substantial brick building was constructed beside the cut to accommodate the waterwheel and pumps and a four-storey water tower was erected alongside, housing a tank at the top, receiving water pumped from the cut, which then flowed through a pipe to a reservoir at The Trinity, behind the houses at The Cross, by force of gravity.

The tower was a strange mixture of architectural styles, surmounted by Gothick crenellation and studded with Georgian industrial windows, but it had a

The old water works on a postcard dated 26 March 1905. Courtesy of Ron Shuard.

OLD WATER TOWER BARBOURNE. WORCESTER

quaint charm all its own and its ivy-clad promontories protruding above the sky-line soon made it a popular local landmark. An attractive stone bridge was constructed across the cut to the site.

The new water works cost £11,000 to build but hardly provided water on tap, since each area of the city was supplied with water only twice a week, and in 1807 the city council agreed to add a steam engine to pump water from the river

The old water tower and adjoining buildings, after their conversion to living accommodation. Courtesy of Clive Haynes.

at the lower end of Pitchcroft. In 1823 the works was taken over by commissioners appointed under a new act of parliament.

In 1848 there was a critical report on public health and the water supply in Worcester, which was hardly surprising to anyone who had got within sniffing distance of the area around the water works. The city fathers had decided that the area was also suitable for waste disposal and the manure heaps - comprising road and stable refuse as well as human waste - were sited right next to the water supply!

Something drastic had to be done, and in 1858 a new waterworks opened, designed by Thomas Hawksley, then still a relatively young man but later to be accounted the greatest expert of his day. The new works had a steam-powered beam engine which pumped water up 160 feet to a reservoir on Rainbow Hill which supplied the city.

This might have seemed better but in fact it was simply a more efficient way to supply citizens with what was still largely untreated water straight from the river, which also carried sewage and industrial waste. Three filter tanks, filtering water through layers of sand and gravel, formed part of the new water works but these proved insufficient to meet the demands of the city.

Even when the city medical officer proposed more effective filtration in 1884 it took ten years to be implemented, after which there was a massive reduction in cases of typhoid.

Worcester historian Bill Gwilliam said that in the 1880s the area around the water tanks was laid out as gardens accessible to the public, providing the district's first public park.

To supplement the Rainbow Hill

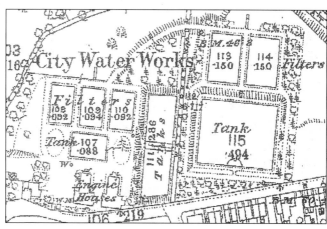

The water works in 1884

reservoir another was dug on Elbury Hill, but the pumps could not cope with the double load, so electric pumps were installed and new steam pumps in 1902 at a cost of £6,440, with almost as much again being spent on additional filtration and a new bridge over Barbourne Brook. At that time Worcester had 46,600 water consumers and there were 72 miles of water mains and 880 fire hydrants.

By the 1990s the water works covered double their original area and had six-teen sand filters and a chemical treatment plant but that did not prevent a con-tamination scare in 1994 when the city's water supply had a distinct scent of something like paraffin. The water supply was quickly declared safe - if boiled - but it was the beginning of the end for the ageing plant and the water works closed in 1995.

When the buildings of the original Barbourne water works became redundant, either in the 1850s or possibly even in the 1820s, the old tower and water works buildings were converted to living accommodation and the cut gradually silted up and had disappeared from maps by 1928. The old buildings continued in use as accommodation for a century or more.

One of the tower's occupants during the late nineteenth century was the artist Harry Jarrmann who painted a charming, if somewhat idealised, view of the old riverside Pope Iron Inn in 1895, shortly before it was demolished. He subse-quently committed suicide in the tower.

The tower, which is still remembered by the street name Tower Road, was taken down in 1957, leaving only the base. The tower site was originally beside the cut but is now beside the brook which has since been diverted back to some-thing like its original course and away from Waterworks Road, after it was found to be causing damage to the foundations of houses there. The site and buildings of the 1858 water works were purchased by the city council in 2000 and are now an environmental centre.

Barbourne Grange the large Georgian house at the junction of the Ombersley and Northwick Roads, partly occupied by a motor accessories shop, may be on a site anciently occupied by the Anglo-Saxon inhabitants of Barbourne.

'Grange' denoted a grain store in ancient times and where the name is found today it often signifies a farm of some antiquity. Its farming roots seem to be con-firmed by a map of the area in about 1880, which shows the Grange and out-buildings surrounded by fields.

Aspects of the construction also suggest a farmhouse rather than a gentle-man's country retreat; the exterior has a solid Georgian brick front but some inte-rior walls are of broken brick. Upper rooms, which would have housed servants quarters, contain reclaimed timbers which could have come from elsewhere, but may also have been re-used from an earlier building on the site.

Records trace the present building back to 1806 though it must be of an ear-lier date, probably late eighteenth century, and it has long been associated with two nearby cottages, originally no doubt for farm workers, which appear much older. The antiquity of settlement on the site seems to be confirmed by the fair-ly recent discovery of a glass bottle at one of the cottages which was dated to around 1650, probably the date of their construction. This is likely therefore to have been the site of a farmhouse and associated buildings for many centuries past.

The deeds held by the present owner of the Grange date only from 1880 but contain an abstract of previous transactions dating back to the beginning of the nineteenth century, which includes a number of names familiar from other land-holdings in the area. The earliest record, an indenture of 1806, was for purchase of the house, which was obviously therefore in existence prior to that date, from members of the Heywood family by John Pearkes Lavender of Lavender House, one of the founders of the Farley, Lavender, Owen and Gutch bank, situated where the Nat West bank now stands on The Cross.

In September 1830 a George Macquay, probably an investor, and Maria Henrietta Cookes of the family which owned Barbourne House, were involved in an indenture for purchase of the property from Lavender, who just four years earlier was being sued by the Cookes family for altering the course of Barbourne Brook.

In November 1853 the property was purchased by John Matthew Gutch, a fellow bank founder with Lavender, though both men had apparently got out before the bank failed in the 1850s. The Grange, with farmland stretching back to Lavender Road and bounded on the west by the Severn, is shown on a map of 1880 when the whole estate was being sold in six lots by the executors of Gutch's deceased widow, Mrs Mary Gutch, who with her sister Miss Jane Lavender had funded building of St Stephen's Church and school in the 1860s.

The Rev T.G. Curtler, himself a substantial landowner in the area and one of the executors of Mrs Gutch's estate, was the first vicar of St Stephen's and stabled his horse at the Grange when visiting the school, in which he took a great interest.

Barbourne Grange

The estate was purchased for £2,836 by another of the executors, Edwin Nicholls, a furniture broker who had established a property company, Worcester Land & Investment, and already owned property in Checketts Lane. The surrounding fields were

101.

then developed for housing but the Grange and the adjoining cottages remained in the hands of the Nicholls family and passed to Edwin Nicholls' daughter, Ellen Mary, on his death in 1899.

She sold the house at auction at the Star Hotel on 27 March 1906, when it was described as having "stabling, coach-house, outbuildings and large gardens comprising lawn and shrubbery with summer house and productive kitchen garden".

The sale catalogue details a large entrance hall, dining room and two kitchens, one with "city water tap", on the ground floor and at first floor level four bedrooms, a drawing room with Sienna marble chimney piece and a WC. Above were two attics with servants quarters but no WC - the servants had to go outside in the yard. There were also two cellars, one vaulted and probably pre-dating the present house. The adjoining cottages were sold separately in the same sale.

Because the house was let on rental, rather than leasehold or copyhold, there are almost no records of who actually occupied it. Only two tenants are known; a Mrs Strode, who was renting the house and garden around 1880 when the estate was sold, and Uriah Robert Cosford, who is shown in the 1906 sales details as having been tenant there for 20 years.

The house was purchased in 1944 by the Harper family who have owned it since and ran a grocery/greengrocery shop there for some years. The gardens may have been used during the war by youngsters from St Stephen's School for growing vegetables. Then or later Spicers builders occupied the yard. One outbuilding, possibly a coach house contemporary with the house, still remains on the site. We are grateful to Laurence Harper for information on the house and estate.

The Yeomanry Riding School

The area had a number of military connections. It was the home of the Worcester Militia, which has already been dealt with under St George's Square, where they were based. This organisation was quite separate from the Worcestershire Regiment, which encamped on Pitchcroft during WW1 and had wooden stabling there. The other military unit based in the area was the Worcestershire Yeomanry, also quite separate from the county regiment. The Yeomanry had a riding school next door to the Barbourne Works at Northwick. They later became a cavalry regiment and were called hussars. Their colonel was the Earl of Dudley, and other members of the county land-owning aristocracy were also involved. It became a parachute regiment during WW11 and was at Arnhem. It has now been swallowed up within a larger TA regiment. The riding school, for information on which we are grateful to Tim Bridges, collections officer at the city's Museums and Art Gallery, became a biscuit packing factory and later the premises of a paint supplier. The building was knocked down about 16 years ago and houses now stand on the site.

Some Local Businesses

Because Barbourne was largely rural in character and then quickly became residential in the nineteenth century it was never an area with a large number of industrial or commercial undertakings, but there were some distinctive businesses in and around the area, some of which have left their mark on it, though others have surprisingly vanished without trace. The selection here, listed south to north, probably includes all of those which are of particular interest.

McNaught's Carriage Works must undoubtedly have been the business best known in its day, since it had an international reputation for the quality of its products.

The works and showrooms were based in the Tything, where one of the former Kays buildings now stands on the corner of St Oswald's Road, but the company also had showrooms at 10 Park Lane, London and in Liverpool and Birmingham, and was a massive exporter of carriages.

The business, founded and run for half a century by James Aldren McNaught (right), who lived at the Langdales in Barbourne Terrace, exhibited the 'prize chariot' at the Great Exhibition of 1851. The firm mostly built state coaches, including many for Indian princes, and in 1887 it built a coach for the Lord Mayor of London which was maintained annually at the Worcester works. All parts of the carriages were made at the factory in Worcester.

The interior of McNaught's carriage works - 1890s

Sadly fire struck the site in the 1890s, which proved disastrous for the firm, with a large part of the premises being destroyed and major financial losses. This came just at the time when the motor car had begun to replace the carriage. The firm made the decision to build cars instead of carriages and supplied many of their products

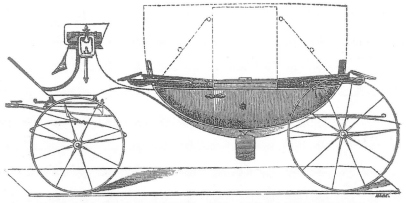

An 1869 advertisement for McNaught's carriages

104.

to visiting dignitaries. They also made ambulances for the military during the first world war, but motor vehicles did not prove as profitable as carriages and the company was wound up in 1918.

Mr McNaught's son continued as a coachbuilder and motor mechanic, with a showroom in Foregate Street and a workshop in Farrier Street, until his death in 1934 and Mr NcNaught's daughter Heera lived in Northwick Close and worshipped for many years at St Stephen's Church.

After the business closed, McNaught's sadly vanished without trace, except for the name McNaught Place, a small entry into what was the Kay's car park, but an interesting footnote to its history is that a company set up by a former employee is still in existence. Scottish coach builder Thomas Carmichael, who appears to have been living in York Place in 1861, worked for a time at McNaughts before striking out on his own at premises in The Butts.

Carmichael's eventually moved part of their operations to premises at Gregory's Mill Street, which became redundant when the company went into administration in 1992, and the factory was derelict for some years until the site was redeveloped for housing.

Thomas Carmichael's family ceased to have any involvement with the company in 1992 but, at the time of writing, it is still going strong making fire engines in Weir Lane, Worcester.

William Forsyth of The Tything was a carver of stone and other materials, whose fine work was a

A McNaught's advertisement from 1910

feature of the Worcester City and County Bank, one of the earliest joint stock banks. which was originally in Foregate Street.

In 1861 a striking new building with classical frontage was built near The Cross, with interior carved work throughout by William Forsyth. In 1889 it amalgamated with Lloyds bank, but the original name, which was no doubt carved by Forsyth, is still visible on the granite facade.

His firm is probably best known though for its connection to one of his apprentices, H H Martyn. Martyn, of Worcester, earned himself a worldwide reputation for his brilliant work after his apprenticeship.

By 1914 he had set up an architectural decorating business in Cheltenham and was employing some 400 workers. He carried out work at Buckingham Palace, which earned him the title of Architectural Decorator to the King. He also did work at Stanbrook Abbey Church, Callow End, the altar piece in the Jesus Chapel in Worcester Cathedral and work at Battenhall Mount.

During the First World War, Martyn's firm was commissioned to produce aircraft parts and by 1918 the firm was producing entire aircraft. These were the early operations of the Gloucester Aircraft Company and until 1928 all the aircraft work was done at the Cheltenham factory.

Worcester Brewery would have been, you might have thought, the most popular business to open in the area, but that was far from true at first.

It had been founded by 1851, when it was shown on a map, on a substantial site on the west side of Barbourne Road, opposite what is now Shrubbery Avenue, under the name Britannia Brewery, presumably from its proximity to Britannia Square, though it is shown in later documents as the Worcester Brewery.

It is thought to have been the first public brewery in Worcester, but the attachment of locals to the traditional ales brewed by the pubs, as they had been for centuries, meant that trade was slow at first. The brewery was originally owned by the Josiah Stallard wine and spirit business, which then operated the Worcester Distillery on South Quay and the wine cellars in Copenhagen Street, near where a descendant of the company operates today.

Planning records show that the brewery, which then had seven licensed houses, was taken over by the Spreckley brothers, who were said to be from London, in 1871. They continued to use the Worcester Brewery name but it was more often known as Spreckley's Brewery. Arthur, one of the Spreckley brothers, lived nearby at Britannia Villa, next door to Thorneloe House.

The brothers boasted that they had trebled the brewery's business after their takeover, but it was not their business acumen alone which was responsible for this; they were fortunate to take over just at the time when traditional prejudice to brewery ales was fading away as more landlords moved over to stocking them.

Nevertheless the brothers invested to encourage growth and they were respon-

Spreckley's Brewery, showing the tower. Courtesy of Ron Shuard.

sible for a number of new buildings on the site, including the brewery tower, a well-known local landmark for many years, which was built in the late nineteenth century. At its greatest extent, the brewery covered some three acres and was the largest in the district.

Barley was purchased mainly from local farmers and malted on site, the malt houses being built at the back of the site towards York Place. Stables were built at about the same time as the malt houses and the site had its own cooperage.

The main business entrance to the site was at the bottom of York Place where separate gates, roughly level with frontages of properties on the east side of the street and running across what is now the road into Windmill Close, gave access to pedestrians and to delivery vehicles.

The brewery produced mild, bitter and stout, sold in barrels and bottles, and by the end of the century they had a bottling plant which could fill 2,500 bottles an hour. They also produced substantial quantities of mineral water, bottled on site, and they took over the old-established wine and spirit business of Joseland & Sons at 7 Foregate Street in 1897.

In June of that year the brewery, with 40 freehold and 17 leasehold licensed properties, and the Joseland business, was sold to a new private company, Spreckley Brothers Ltd., for the substantial sum of £150,000. They also supplied free houses as well as supplying direct to the public; in 1903 a gallon of Spreckley's Harvest Beer cost 6d (about 2.5p).

Spreckley's Brewery dray for crate deliveries. Courtesy of Ron Shuard.

There was a fire watcher's post at the top of the brewery tower during the second world war and the tower also housed a Home Guard arms store. A few years after the war the tower was struck by lightning during a terrific thunderstorm.

With hindsight this might be seen as an ill omen for the brewery, since in 1958 it was taken over, along with 67 tied houses, by Cheltenham & Hereford Breweries and within two years it had closed. Cheltenham & Hereford, renamed West Country Breweries, was itself taken over by Whitbread five years later.

After Spreckley's Brewery closed the buildings were derelict for many years, but some, including the impressive oast house, were eventually converted into a housing development. Opposite Shrubbery Avenue is a building which was originally a pumping engine house and later a bottling plant, which stands today as a monument to the quality of Victorian industrial building.

St George's Laundry

A little way down St George's Lane, on the south side, was the Steam Laundry which had an impressive frontage onto St George's Square (pictured previously), although the business entrance was at the rear in the lane.

In 1878 the laundry purchased the former Worcester Militia base, described in notes on St George's Square. Later they also had a sports field for employees by Pound Walk. Within twenty years they were referred to as the Worcester and Malvern Sanitary Laundry and 17 years later were advertising themselves as the Worcester and Malvern Steam Laundry and Carpet Beating Company.

Around the turn of the century they enterprisingly produced postcards for distribution to existing and potential clients, pre-printed with their address and the message "Please send Van for Parcel and oblige"; the customer just filled in their name and address and posted it.

A postcard in the possession of Worcester collector Ron Shuard has the address of a customer in Malvern and the company made collections in many of the outlying villages as well as three days a week in the city, using horse-drawn and, by 1915, motor vans.

The laundry also had branches further afield around the country and so laundry was brought into Barbourne from far and wide.

Martin Smith, originally from Somers Road, recalls that during the second world war Americans based in Worcestershire brought their laundry there to be done and threw sweets to youngsters in the St George's School playground, which must have been a real treat for children growing up with rationing.

The laundry was owned by a family called Armstrong but run by a manager; J Davenport was managing the business in 1898.

People who used the laundry from time to time recall it still being open in 1982 but it had closed by 1985, no doubt the victim of laundrettes and domestic washing machines, and flats now stand on the site.

THE WORCESTER AND MALVERN
Steam Laundry and Carpet Beating Company, Ltd.,

Dyers and Dry Cleaners

ST. GEORGE'S LANE, WORCESTER.

Washings Collected on receipt of Post Card.

Our Motor and Horse Vans collect in Worcester and District:

MONDAY.—Worcester, Fernhill Heath, Droitwich and District, Callow End, Malvern Link, Colwall, Great Malvern and District.

TUESDAY.—Worcester, Whittington, Kempsey, Great Malvern.

WEDNESDAY.—Worcester, Spetchley, Stoulton, Pinvin, Pershore, Defford, Upton-on-Severn, Severn Stoke.

THURSDAY.—Droitwich, Hadley, Ombersley, Holt, Witley Court, Hallow, Bransford, Leigh Sinton, Leigh Court.

MAY WE COLLECT YOUR LAUNDRY WORK, CARPETS, DYEING AND CLEANING, BEDS AND MATTRESSES.

Tel. 148 Worcester.   *Managing Director—G. W. ARMSTRONG.*

A 1910 advertisement

Gregory's Mill was a grist mill built originally by William Frebara, Master of St Oswald's Hospital, in 1369, though it was not then known by that name. It stood near Barbourne Brook, about half a mile upstream from Barbourne Bridge.

The mill must have been rebuilt in the seventeenth century since a document of 1659 notes that the mills of Barbourne had been demolished, perhaps in the civil war. Where or how many there were the document does not say, but there was certainly either a corn mill or an iron mill shown on a 1751 map in what is now Gheluvelt Park. It was a large building of two bays which sat astride the brook. All traces of it had gone by 1838, but for a waterfall which still remains.

At some time, Thomas Gregory rented the mill on the brook and since then the area where it stood has always been known as Gregory's Mill. Worcester historian Bill Gwilliam suggested, at various times, both the seventeenth and nineteenth centuries for Gregory's occupation of the site and

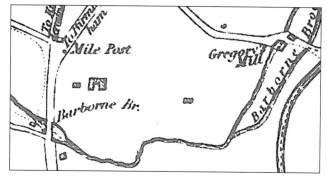

The location of Gregory's Mill on a map of about 1840

his confusion is understandable, since there appears to be no direct documentary evidence in existence to prove the exact date.

If Mr Gregory began his tenancy in the nineteenth century it must have been quite early in that century since the mill is shown under the name of Gregory's Mill on a map of about 1830 and it was given that name in a landscape painted before 1825. On the whole, an earlier date than the nineteenth century seems likely, perhaps some time in the eighteenth century.

The mill, as depicted on a plan of 1751, was powered by water from the brook which was diverted to the mill by way of a leat or channel into two large head ponds, which supplied water to the wheel chamber under the mill. The water ran out through the tail race and along a channel to rejoin the brook further downstream.

In the eighteenth century the brook was much wider immediately to the east of Barbourne Bridge than it is today, perhaps to accommodate the increased flow when the mill was working and the stream was swollen by water from the tail race leat. A painting from before 1825, the only known illustration of the mill, shows the mill as a half-timbered building with a substantial brick addition at one end, perhaps providing living accommodation for the miller and his family.

The only known illustration of Gregory's Mill, a painting from the Prattinton Collection, completed around 1825. Courtesy of the Society of Antiquaries.

The mill was still grinding corn in the First World War but it ceased to operate in 1919, probably unable to cope with competition from steam-powered mills, and had been demolished by 1950 so completely that we have been unable to find any remains. Mr Gwilliam believed that one wall of the mill still survived in 1970 as part of a workshop, but there have been many changes in this area even in just the past 35 years.

The watercourses, which had been diverted from the brook to feed the water-wheel at the mill and the two mill ponds, have been filled in leaving no physical remains but the mill must undoubtedly have been the longest lived local business and it is remembered in two nearby street names.

The lane leading to the mill was known simply as Mill Lane as late as 1874 but by 1896 it had been changed to Gregory's Mill Street. The name Gregory's Bank is much older, having been in use in the early nineteenth century and shown on a map of 1830.

Pope Iron must rate as the most mysterious Barbourne business. This ironworks, which revived the old Roman tradition of ironmaking in the area, has given its name to a road and a pub just beyond the north end of Pitchcroft, but little is known about it.

It is believed, by Worcester historian Bill Gwilliam, to have been founded in the eighteenth century by Bromwich Pope. He notes that in 1751 a Bromwich Pope and his wife Mrs Mercy Pope owned a forge on Dick Brook, about six miles up the Severn.

The Pope Iron works were situated on Barbourne Brook and the east bank of the Severn, presumably bringing in iron ore and timber for smelting by river, perhaps from the Forest of Dean as the Romans had. The works are shown covering a substantial riverside site on a landholding plan of 1808 but had apparently gone, or at least ceased working, by 1880 when houses were built across the riverside slipway, though the first directory of residents of Waterworks Road in 1884 included at least one iron worker.

In the late 1890s the original half-timbered riverside tavern, which may also have been eighteenth century and would have served river travellers as well as iron workers, was taken down and a New Pope Iron pub was built on the site it still occupies today in Pope Iron Road, though it has recently been renamed The Winning Post.

The first inn of that name was photographed, and was painted in its original position on the riverside in 1895 just before it was taken down, when it was kept by a Mrs Teague. The artist was Harry Jarrmann who apparently lived in the old waterworks tower and later committed suicide there.

Ten houses forming part of Waterworks Road were built alongside the Severn on the site of the old pub in 1896 - 8 by a Mr Rowlands who apparently was, or had been, a missionary. The lane leading to the site from Barbourne Road became Waterworks Road by 1884 and the lane approaching it from the south is now the north entrance to Pitchcroft.

The area of what is now Gheluvelt Park had waterfalls and three pools, including one on the site of the present tennis courts, which must have been intended to ensure a steady water supply to the ironworks.

The old Pope Iron inn on the riverside. Courtesy of Ron Shuard.

Ward's Barbourne Leather Works may rate as the smelliest Barbourne business because of some of the weird and not so wonderful 'raw materials' used in its processes. It was founded in 1892 by businessman J.R.H. Ward on the Severn side of Pope Iron Road, at its junction with Pitchcroft Lane.

We have no information on his life before he set up the business, but he seems not to have been a tanner by trade and there was a successful late nineteenth century ironmongers and heating and sanitary engineers called J. Ward & Son at 21 Broad Street, with which he may have been connected.

The leather industry had once made Worcester a thriving industrial centre in the sixteenth and early seventeenth centuries and the largest city in the West Midlands at that time. By the nineteenth century the industry was not the force it had been but there were still four large glove makers and no doubt many smaller ones, plus boot and shoe makers in the city, and a number of tanners and leather

Ward's massive leather works in Pope Iron Road, Barbourne, pictured in 1903. Courtesy of Martin Smith.

dressers, and fellmongers (dealers in animal carcasses and hides) operating mainly in St John's, though there was an old established tannery on the canalside between the Blockhouse and George Street which utilised water from three local springs, and the massive Fownes glove factory tanned many of its own hides.

The establishment of Ward's Barbourne works may have been the first instance of the tanning trade operating north of the city, but this must have been a good site with ample water supplies.

The works expanded exponentially and John Ward moved in 1897 from a three-storey terraced house at No. 2 Barbourne Terrace around the corner to a larger and more modern house, Woodhall, in Sabrina Terrace, where a near neighbour was Frank Bayliss of the well-known printing company which still thrives at the top of London Road. But the strain of building a fast-growing business must have been considerable and around 1900 John Ward died.

Much of the technical expertise in tanning was supplied from the first by Thomas William Badgery who ran a glove leather business in the city, and must have been from the family of Badgerys who began as fell mongers but progressed to leather dressing, with premises in various locations in St John's for many years past. When Ward died, Badgery took over as Managing Director and the family afterwards remained in charge throughout the existence of the company, though it always retained the Ward name.

Within eleven years of their establishment, the works had increased to four times their original size and photographs taken at that time for a business supplement published by the Worcester Daily Times show substantial and distinctive three-storey buildings extending back ninety yards from the junction with Pitchcroft Lane to almost opposite what was then the New Pope Iron pub. It was hardly surprising that the company proudly displayed a line drawing of its premises on its letterhead.

Despite the odours the works emitted, they were very much at the quality end

**Ward's were so proud of their extensive works that
they put an illustration of them on their letterhead**

of the market, producing many leathers which would have been used in the most expensive shoes. At the turn of the century the company was said to be importing 3,000 calf skins each week from France, 6,000 goat skins from the East Indies (probably Indonesia) and 2,000 sheep skins from South Africa and Arabia.

They described themselves as manufacturers of quality leathers rather than tanners, and boasted they were the European pioneers of 'chrome tanning' for boot uppers, a process still sometimes used, in which leather is treated with chromium to make it harder and more resistant to heat. Their literature noted that their products included "the celebrated 'Severn', 'Moor' and 'Castle' calf in black and colours and 'Cabinet' and 'Khartum' glace" - glace being fine kid leather for gloves and shoes which was specially coated and polished with a glass ball.

They also diversified into leather for gloves, again producing high quality calf used in evening dress wear as well as leather for everday gloves and, with an eye to a new and expanding market, special tanned leather for driving gloves.

The company prided itself on being equipped with the latest, mostly American, machinery. It generated its own gas on the premises to drive three gas

Inside Ward's leather works, 1903. Courtesy of Martin Smith.

engines which were then described as "powerful" though they had a combined rating of only 175 horse power. The works were lit by gas and had lifts and even an automatic sprinkler system, but although the ventilation system was described as "excellent" it just couldn't do anything about that smell!

Nearby residents with long memories recall the works as "smelly" and that's hardly surprising, considering what was used to treat the hides. Martin Smith, whose family had a haulage business in Somers Road, recalls going with his dad as a teenager to collect salt from Stoke Works, Droitwich; dog 'muck' from hound kennels at Fernhill Heath and bullocks' blood from the slaughter house near the Infirmary, all of which was delivered to Wards for treatment of hides.

The salt was used in the initial soak in huge vats, presumably to soften the hides, and blood and dog 'muck' soaks were probably used for dying. Hides were then forced through massive rolling machines to stretch them before they went into a drying room and were then passed back and forth through another machine to glaze them, though that is an over-simplification of the processing involved, since every hide was said to go through 48 different processes on its way through the works.

Brenda Martin, who worked there trimming hides from before the second world war until 1946 when she married, recalled that the smell was so dreadful she felt too sick to eat when she got home in the evenings. Daughter Glenys, who later went with mum to take sandwiches to dad, who was in charge of maintenance, remembers it as very dark and noisy inside.

The company had originally sold a great deal of its boot leather through its large warehouse in Leicester but, from the beginning, export markets had been vital. At the turn of the century Europe, Australia and South Africa were important markets and Mrs Martin believes that the factory's output at the time she worked there, around WW II, was all exported to America.

At that time Bill Badgery was in charge and his nephew Alec, who lived in Ombersley Road, had joined the business, which was apparently as buoyant as ever, but perhaps cheap foreign imports in the 1960s and 70s created impossible competition, as they did for so many other companies.

Whatever the reason, Wards had closed by 1978, and Alec and his son Eddie opened and operated a new tanning business for a time at the other end of Pope Iron Road. Sadly Wards' distinctive Victorian buildings were demolished and replaced with a series of mostly nondescript industrial units.

Barbourne Nurseries must have been the largest local business in terms of land area. At its greatest extent it occupied the area between Sunnyside Road and Perdiswell, bounded on the east by the brook and on the west by Ombersley Road.

For around two centuries the nurseries grew apples, pears and plums and produced perry, cider and cyder, the connoisseur's version of the drink. The business was owned by Lord Foley in 1751 and later by the Wakemans of Perdiswell Hall, but it was usually let to and operated by a nurseryman who lived at a property which still stands on Droitwich Road near Beech Avenue.

In 1896 the nurseryman was William Rowe who had a shop at 65 Broad Street and other outlets in Barbourne, Claines and Droitwich. His foreman, J. Carless, was responsible for a new apple variety, William Crump, based on the Worcester Permain of Smith's Nurseries in St John's, and Rowes also introduced a variety called Edward VII in 1908.

Cottages were built for the many workers who must have been needed; a row of nursery cottages still stands in Checketts Lane and there are others elsewhere around the area. There were also reportedly old fruit trees in the gardens of new-built houses in Ombersley Road in the 1880s and 90s, suggesting that they had survived the conversion from nursery land to residential area. The nurseries still existed in 1928 but the continual urban encroachment led to their final demise.

We are indebted for information on the nurseries to Mrs Madeleine Goodier who has carried out extensive research on them.

Barbourne Works, the substantial late nineteenth century buildings in Northwick Avenue, were originally the premises of printing firm W.E. Tucker & Co. Ltd. and their initials can still be seen on a cartouche above the main

Barbourne Works, pictured in a pamphlet produced by Tucker's

entrance. Mr Tucker was described in the firm's literature as having previously been senior partner in the London printing firm of Tucker, Johnson & Co., but he had been in business for some years at No. 15, Worcester High Street, and successfully so, since on 21 February 1889 he submitted a planning application to extend those premises.

The additional space was apparently not sufficient however, and on 24 January 1898, a planning application was lodged for the Barbourne works and two new roads leading to it, now Northwick and Sabrina Avenues. The three-storey works were planned by Mr Tucker but financed by the Hon. Percy Allsopp.

The works were designed by Briggs of London and constructed by Worcester building firm Bromage and Evans, founded in 1883 in Derby Road, which carried out many other high profile contracts around the area, including building the Hop Market Hotel and "the college for the blind sons of gentlemen" at Whittington, rebuilding the Old Rectifying House and moving Queen Elizabeth's House in the Trinity to its present location. Despite these prestigious commissions they regarded Barbourne Works as one of their largest contracts.

At the front of the works were the administration and despatch departments; the warehouses, packing rooms, artists' rooms, counting house and the book-binding department. Behind this was a massive machinery or print hall which rose the full height of the building with a glass roof above. It was equipped for

The impressive press hall at Tucker's Barbourne Works

letterpress and for lithographic printing and was said to have some of the largest presses in the trade.

It was surrounded by open-plan galleries for processing departments at first and second floor levels. The composing and folding and sewing departments were at first floor level and the transparency, varnishing and gumming departments on the second floor. The works had its own electricity generating plant, fire hydrants and elevators and was well equipped with mess rooms and toilets.

Tuckers boasted that: "No kind of printing escapes our notice, from a wedding card to a prayer book, from a 16-sheet poster to the smallest ticket". As other examples of their versatile product list they quoted: "books, pamphlets, price lists, catalogues, posters, bills, tradesmen's circulars, bazaar programmes, prospectuses, particulars and conditions of sale, also law, bankers', shipping and general merchants' requirements."

They also proudly advertised themselves as "Sole suppliers of Lithoglas window decoration in imitation of stained glass and (for) window advertisements', and boasted, "novelties and modern ideas are constantly emanating from our presses". Large posters were a particular speciality and there was a complete department dedicated solely to their production.

The company must have employed many skilled workers who could not all have come from the Worcester print trade. No doubt Mr Tucker tempted employees away from Birmingham and even London companies by emphasising the advantages of living in Worcester.

In an illustrated pamphlet the company said: "We have no London smoke to contend with; but here we have fresh air, good light, best materials and healthy work-people." The pamphlet also emphasised that "workmen are paid the full Trade Society wages".

Clearly a massive printing operation like this could not hope to survive on the print work available in Worcester and presumably Mr Tucker hoped to take advantage of lower costs in the provinces to cut prices and attract work from London and nationally. If that was his plan, it was a bold idea and one which should have been effective, since finished print work could quickly be despatched to any part of the country by railway.

Perhaps it was an idea ahead of its time or perhaps Mr Tucker simply overreached himself with such a massive plant. At any rate, by 1903 his meticulously planned print works had become a ladies' clothing factory. The buildings were later part of Kays' home shopping operation and recently, after being empty for many years, have been converted into Worcester's newest product - luxury apartments.

PART FOUR
LIFE IN BARBOURNE

The Younger Generation

Some pictures of Barbourne youngsters from the first half of the twentieth century.

Picture on Facing Page :

These youngsters from York Place, pictured about 1925, were ready for a fancy dress party. The picture was taken at the bottom of the street on the east side and just visible behind them is the pedestrian gate to Spreckley's Brewery.

The picture was provided by Mrs Gladys Green of York Place, who amazingly remembers all but one of the names.

Front row, l - r, Thelma Wilmott, Sarah Bennett, not known, Wally Phillips, Jack Budden, Neville Phillips, Lilly Curtiss;

middle row, Freddie Ratcliffe, Dickie, Edgar White, Dickie O'Callaghan, Mrs Green (then Meadows), Tom Price;

back row, Winnie Meadows (Mrs Vale), Nora Phillips (Mrs Smith), Gwen Howell (Mrs Millington).

The next two pictures are of St George's Scouts, who had a scout hut at the bottom of Brook Street. They won both the Spreckley's Shield for under-15s and the Whitely Shield for over-15s. Group scoutmaster in the 1940s was Bert 'Tubby' Davis, a cooper at the vinegar works. St Stephen's also had a scout troop but it closed before the end of the war.

First Picture :

St George's Z Scout Troop, pictured at Brook Street, Barbourne, about 1949. Courtesy of John Smith, who has supplied us with this information :
Back row, Bill Wilson (scout master), Ken Batty, Trever Jones, Graham Avery, John Smith, Martin Smith, Nevill Kennedy, Brian Jones, Jeff Ambrose, Owen Rivett;
middle second row down, Ray Handy (scout master);
on left, Mrs Powell (cub mistress).

Second Picture :

St George's Senior Scout Troop, pictured at Brook Street, Barbourne, about 1949. Courtesy of Martin Smith, who has supplied us with this information :

Back row, Ken Batty, Nevill Kennedy, Ray Handy (scout master), Jeff Ambrose, Owen Rivett;
front row, John Smith, Martin Smith, Graham Avery, Brian Jones, Tutter Speaks, Trever Jones.

Gheluvelt Park

The park was originally the private estate of Barbourne House, which was actually more extensive than the present park. Before it was purchased by Worcester City Council in 1920 it was known as Great Park and formed the private grounds of Barbourne College.

The park forms part of the City of Worcester's memorial to the First World War. It is named after the Belgian village where the 2nd Battalion, Worcestershire Regiment, lost 189 men and three officers while preventing the German army from reaching the Channel ports and turning the Allied line in October 1914.

Gheluvelt was a weak point in a thinly-defended British line, and on the morning of 31 October 1914 the Germans launched a powerful offensive and by early afternoon had captured the village, killing most of the British troops, except for a couple of small pockets of defenders holding out at the chateau.

The 350 Worcestershire men and six officers under Major E.B. Hankey, who won the VC for this action, were in reserve and had spent a miserable night in a nearby wood, but they quickly launched a counter-attack.

**Col. Hankey
Courtesy of
Worcester
News**

One hundred men or more were killed or wounded by shelling as they crossed the open ground from the wood to the village, but they pressed on and their attack took the Germans by surprise and forced them out of the village.

A Worcesters private wrote in his diary: "The Germans fled in a solid, grey mass. We plugged the gap to Calais". The engagement was referred to by the British commander, Field Marshall Sir John French, who was later to open the park, as "the most critical moment of the whole of this great battle of Ypres".

He added: "If any one unit can be singled out for special praise, it is the Worcestershires". But the achievement came at a terrible price - the 2nd Battalion lost more than half its strength in that one engagement.

Gheluvelt Park was used as industrial land in 1751 by a Mr Richard Garway for his business, which was listed as sail cloth making, but he is also listed as being bankrupt.

It has been suggested that the land could have been a whitening yard and that a building straddling the brook, in the middle of the park, could have been a mill. Mr Garway rented the land from Mr Cookes.

The house was home to Rev Thomas Cookes in 1778, and had been in the hands of the Cookes family since the early sixteenth century. On the site were several pools, which could have been used for the dying of cloth and the brook was an excellent source for the large volumes of water which the business would consume. So we know that the land was in some kind of industrial use in the mid 1700s and that the business relied heavily on large amounts of water and large pools to carry out its work.

Barbourne House was said to have been rebuilt in the late eighteenth century. Mr J.P. Lavender lived in a property on what was later known as Lavender Road and also owned property on the other side of Barbourne House, running down to the Severn. In 1838, he purchased the Cookes property and changed the boundary between Lavender Road and the park.

In 1879, Barbourne House was listed as Barbourne Villa, but has not been referred to as that before or since. Barbourne Brook was once at the centre of a bitter legal battle, due to the then owner, John Parkes Lavender Esq., changing the course of the brook.

In 1826 Lavender Road, which runs alongside the park, was a private carriage road and a section where the road widens into a semi-circle was a turning area for carriages taking their occupants to the house. By 1928 the park keeper's house was listed as being at No. 1 Lavender Road.

The old Swan Public House stood on an island, which was formed by the Brook, in 1774. The pub has since been rebuilt and modernised to the hostelry we

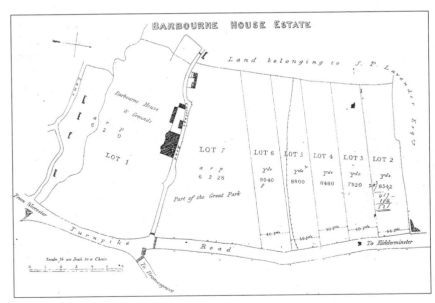

The Barbourne House estate when it was being sold at auction in 1837

128.

see today. The original Swan was said to have been a picturesque, old-fashioned place.

It appears that the site was turned into pleasure grounds in about 1830, with three fishponds, lawns, shrubberies and a network of paths. When the estate was for sale in 1879, it was described as: "Lawn, and pleasure grounds, tastefully laid out, fishponds, bridges, shrubbery with terrace walks and summer houses."

As a result of this sale Barbourne House was turned into a school and for some years was known as Barbourne College, which is dealt with in more detail later.

In 1885 a programme of improvements was implemented for the bridge area which involved raising and widening the bridge and the surrounding road. The road surface was raised by 1m at this time.

By 1909, the park was for sale again, and was described as having: "attractive grounds, (well timbered with Oak, Elm, Birch, Beech, Poplar, Ash, Chestnut, Fir and other trees), and of inclining elevation towards Barbourne Brook, a stream of exceptionally clear water. Includes Paddock, Tennis and Croquet Lawns, Lake, Open air swimming bath with diving board.

"There is an extensive vegetable and fruit garden, walled in on three sides, facing south, warm and very productive, well stocked with a good variety of fruit trees. The garden buildings include glass house and in the rear yard are fowl pens, apple store and a pig stye etc."

Also on the site at this time were several temporary buildings being used as classrooms, a laboratory and a gymnasium. Occasionally during the park's time as a college the gardens were opened to the public, and open air productions of Shakespeare plays were performed. The estate remained unsold.

In 1912, W. P, Caldwell, headmaster of Barbourne College, offered the land for sale for the sum of £3,000. In 1916 the land was for sale again, this time for £2,400. On 9th February 1918 the land was sold to the corporation of Worcester for £2,328.

Barbourne College was demolished to make way for a row of memorial houses. The houses, dedicated to the memory of those killed in the Battle of Gheluvelt and to be occupied by ex-servicemen,

GHELUVELT PARK.

OPENING BY EARL OF YPRES,

City's Freedom for Distingu'shed Soldier.

Worcester gave a cordial welcome to Earl Yprés on Saturday when he attended to open Gheluvelt Park, the new recreation ground which is so designated to mark the signal achievement of the 2nd Worcesters in October, 1914.

The Earl of Ypres came into the City from Madresfield, where he had been staying with Earl Beauchamp. They were met at the City boundary by Col. A. T. Anderson, who commands the Royal Artillery of the 48th Division, and is the senior serving officer in the county. So escorted, the Earl of Ypres proceeded to the Guildhall, where already a large company had assembled at the Mayor's invitation to meet their noble guest.

The Assembly.

Those who accepted invitations of the Mayor and Mayoress were :—
Members of the Corporation : The High Sheriff and Mrs. P. J. Roberts, the City Chamberlain :Mr. R. Haughton) Ald. and Mrs. J. S.

The opening of Gheluvelt Park. reported by Berrow\s Joural on 24 June 1922

These grainy but fascinating images are taken from a unique film record of the opening of Gheluvelt Park, courtesy of Brian Hewlett, whose grandad had one of the earliest cinemas in Worcester, the Apollo in Park Street.

The pictures show (facing page) Field Marshall Sir John French, the Earl of Ypres, arriving at the park with civic dignitaries and on the platform, the massive crowds (above) and Worcesters veterans attending the event, below.

were originally to be built on Rainbow Hill but the committee promoting their construction approached the council in April 1918 and secured the location in Barbourne.

The foundation stone for the houses was laid in 1919 and the first houses were completed by the following year.

On Saturday June 17th 1922, Field Marshall Earl French, the Earl of Ypres, officially opened the park during a day of celebration which literally brought the city to a halt and graphically illustrated the pride which citizens clearly felt at the dedication of such a major memorial to their fallen heroes.

Seven thousand men from the city went to fight, 500 of whom never returned. The number of those who returned broken in spirit or body is not recorded, but at least the homes for ex-servicemen were making some practical provision for those who had survived the war.

The Earl had spent the previous night as the guest of Earl Beauchamp at Madresfield Court and on Saturday morning he received a military escort from the city boundary to the Guildhall where the Worcestershire Regiment had mounted an honour guard. The High Street, then a traffic route, was closed for the occasion and a crowd of 50,000 people gathered to cheer the Earl's arrival.

Inside the Guildhall a large company of city and county dignitaries had gathered for a lunch at which the Mayor, Samuel Southall - after whom a secondary

This picture, courtesy of Ron Shuard, shows his grandad, Jim Griffiths, preparing to cut the grass in Gheluvelt Park with a scythe in the early 1920s. Despite strenuous efforts, Ron has never been able to identify the young man

school was later named in Merriman's Hill Road - presented the Earl with the freedom of the city.

Afterwards the assembled company made its way north along Barbourne Road, closed off for the occasion at the Ombersley Road/Droitwich Road junction, led by the honour guard and the regimental band. There were so many dignitaries that only the most important could be transported by car; the rest had to travel by tram.

Crowds lined the route and thousands more packed the park hours before the scheduled arrival of the platform party at 3pm. Berrow's Worcester Journal described the "tremenduous burst of cheering" that greeted the Earl's arrival, which he acknowledged with a smart military salute before accepting a gift of a gold key with which to unlock the park gates.

The Earl spoke in praise of the Worcestershire regiment and the city's war work and congratulated the city on its choice of memorial, which, he said, would be "of the greatest advantage and the utmost utility". It would not only provide citizens with rest and enjoyment after the day's work but would be "a constant

This tank was a popular feature of the park for many years. Ron Shuard, who provided this picture, says it arrived on the day the park opened in 1922 and was broken up for scrap in 1940 when metal was in short supply. It stood in front of the first bungalow, roughly where a round flower bed is now

Youngsters playing in Gheluvelt Park in the 1920s. Courtesy of Ron Shuard.

reminder to them of what Worcestershire men had been". The ceremonies were concluded with a tour of the park and the planting of an oak tree on the south side of the park overlooking the brook..

It cost £4,540 for the park to be laid out, including flowerbeds, paddling area and playground. The brook had been cleaned out and the bed concreted in 1921, and a number of bridges were built across it, all of which were originally in a rustic style. In 1922 birds were purchased for a bird sanctuary which was still shown on maps of the park in 1928.

In the early 1920s, the land for the six tennis courts was set aside and in 1923 two of the courts were ready to play on. It is presumed that these were the hard courts. The remaining plots for the grass courts were planted with potatoes to prepare the ground for the laying of the courts. In 1925 chocolate philanthropist Richard Cadbury donated a tea house and a shelter which were placed next to the tennis courts. In 1932 the tennis courts consisted of two hard and four grass courts and cost 9d per person for the hard courts and 6d per person for the grass courts.

In 1923 the bandstand was donated by the High Sheriff. It still stands and is still used occasionally in the summer for performances and concerts. Before the Second World War band performances in the park were always well attended. A photograph from the 1930s shows a large crowd gathered to watch a band perform.

In 1924, play equipment was purchased for the park. This consisted of two sets of swings, two see-saws, a slide and a sand pit. Girls and boys had to use different swings and see-saws, and this is why two of each were purchased. Older residents recall that youngsters received a serious telling-off from the park keeper if they dared use the wrongs swings! There was also a pitch and putt course in the park in the 1930s and in the late 1930s/early 1940s a miniature railway was installed within the park.

In 1964, the brook was found to have been polluted by industrial waste and was fenced off amid concerns for the safety of children who might wish to play in the water. This brought about the building of the paddling pool, which opened shortly afterwards next to the brook. The present paddling pool was installed in the park in 1965 and a picture of it was taken on Christmas Day 1965, when it had been built but was not yet in use. It was the only paddling pool in the city but it has also since closed over fears of pollution.

The park has recently been extended down to the river, but it exists within a very different society from that in which it was founded. Today we tend to prefer to get some fresh air in our own gardens and the pre-war heyday of the park, when it would be packed for Sunday entertainments, is long gone, but it still provides a very pleasant environment for those with time to sit and watch the world go by, and its importance as Barbourne's 'green lung' is beyond price.

The Ferries

There were two river ferries serving Barbourne in the nineteenth and early twentieth centuries, although the dates at which they commenced operation are not clear.

The Kepax ferry, named for nearby Kepax House, was situated just north of where the brook now runs into the Severn and had perhaps been in operation for many years; it was certainly in operation around 1830 when it was shown on a map as Barbourn Ferry.

At the turn of the nineteenth century it was known locally as Bailey's Boat, since the boatman was a Mr Bailey and all the houses around the boatman's house were occupied by his six married daughters!

In 1898, prior to the arrival of the Baileys, the ferry was run by Albert Cheston who lived in Park View Terrace. The old Pope Iron inn, formerly on the riverside, will have served waiting passengers. The ferry probably last ran in the 1940s and is remembered today by the street names Kepax Gardens and Ferry Villas.

The other ferry ran from the Dog and Duck tavern on the far bank of the river, roughly opposite the centre of Pitchcroft, at the bottom of Ferry Bank. Passengers' bags would be transported up the steep bank by donkey. The pub got its name from a barbaric watermen's game in which a duck's wing tendons were cut so that it could not fly and dogs were then set on the terrified bird, with betting on which would catch it.

Pubs were always associated with these ferries since the tidal nature of the

The Dog and Duck ferry in the 1930s. Courtesy of Clive Haynes.

The Kepax ferry, early twentieth century. Courtesy of Clive Haynes.

river meant that once the tide went out the ferry could not operate for some hours and the landlord had a 'captive' clientele. At the Dog and Duck crossing there were once stepping stones to allow people to cross the river on foot at low tide and Ferry Bank was then called Ford Bank. The construction of the lock and weir at Bevere and modern dredging of the river has put an end to this tidal flow. Crossing the river on the Dog and Duck ferry cost 1d. in the 1920s. The tavern had closed by 1929 when the family of the present occupant moved there and his father later took down the long boathouse which can be seen on earlier photographs, although another outbuilding is still there. A photograph of the ferry in 1935 shows that it continued working for some years after the pub closed, finally ceasing operation in the mid 1940s.

Shopping in Barbourne: 1880s - 1900s

The residents of the thriving Victorian suburb needed somewhere to do their shopping. There were many shops lining the Tything and Foregate Street but the area developed its own thriving shopping centre along Barbourne Road and in the streets around it.

Just beyond St George's Square was a store which may have been amongst the earliest shops in the area. George Edward Bond's grocery store was established in a solid Victorian villa called Westwood House, immediately on the north side of St George's Lane North in 1876.

Some 20 years later the premises were photographed with a young man in his late 20s or early 30s, presumably Mr Bond's son, standing in the doorway with a boy in a then fashionable sailor suit beside him, so we undoubtedly have here two generations of the Bond family.

But within a year or two, by 1898, Bond's store had become No. 3 branch of the Worcestershire Co-operative Society. The shop premises on the ground floor were then much enlarged but if you look above, the exterior of Westwood House at first floor level is still essentially as it was when Mr Bond was there, though the interior is much altered and the garden shown in the 1896 photograph has been built over. It closed as a Co-op in the 1970s and is now a tool hire shop.

Opposite Paradise Row from 1864 or earlier was Paradise Place, a row of Victorian villas, which by 1880 had become a parade of shops and has remained so right up to the present day. No. 1, on the corner of Hebb Street, was originally occupied by Miss Brotheridge, a fancy draper, but in 1888 a grocery store opened there to serve residents living at the city end of the suburb and Richardsons' Stores quickly became the place to go for groceries.

The Worcester firm which owned the store had originally set up in business in the Cornmarket early in the nineteenth century, but in 1888 they decided to take

G.E. Bond's grocery store at Westwood House on the corner of St George's Lane North, about 1896. Courtesy of the Co-operative Society.

Above: Richardsons' Stores at No. 1 Barbourne Road, on the corner of Hebb Street. This photograph presumably shows recruits from an outlying area, perhaps Claines, being marched into Worcester early in the first world war. Below: When Hebb Street was widened in the 1960s these cottages there and Richardsons' were demolished. Both pictures courtesy of Ron Shuard.

advantage of the city's expansion by opening two new stores, one in Barbourne and another in St John's. The expansion went so well that two years later they opened two more branches, at Worcester Road, Malvern and Barton Street, Tewkesbury.

The wine and spirit department was a particular feature of the Barbourne store and the company prided itself on its imports of meat from America, Canadian Cheddar cheese and Danish, Swedish and Irish butters. They carried several "exclusive" brands including their 'Meadow Sweet' unsalted Danish butter and 'Goodwins Digestive Self-Raising Flour' and claimed to have gained a particular reputation for their teas which, they said, "are scientifically blended from the choichest leaves" making the stores "by far the largest dealers of tea in the district". Oddly then most Paradise Row traders used The Tything as their address.

The store continued to be a feature of the Barbourne shopping scene for many years but its premises were knocked down when Hebb Street was widened in the 1960s, which is why the numbers in Barbourne Road no longer begin at No. 1.

The other early shops on Paradise Place included the area's own post office at No. 2, run by Miss Price who also sold confectionery. In 1884 there were four collections of mail each day, the first at 9.15am and the last at 7.30pm, with no collections on Sundays. By 1910 this had increased to 11 on weekdays, the first at 8.30am and the last at 11.50pm, with two collections on Sundays.

At No. 3 was the greengrocer's shop of Miss J. Miles whose brother John lived with her above the shop and was a recruiting sergeant, presumably for the Worcestershire Regiment, and next door was the hardware shop of Chas. Jarman.

A nineteenth century ad from the St George's parish magazine. Courtesy of Ian Pattison.

Beyond were the premises of Walter Noake, boot and shoe maker, who boasted he was "the only manufacturer who retails his own made boots". This was a very old-established Barbourne business, founded about 1800, which passed through at least three generations of the family. By 1903 the business had passed to the grandsons of the founder and changed its name to Noake Bros, with shops in the Tything, St Swithin's Street and St John's. They were said to be the largest makers of hand-sewn boots in the county.

The small parade of shops also had Mrs Cockbill a china and glass dealer and

This nineteenth century photograph of Teddy Ranford's shop on the corner of Somers Road has seen better days but we considered it well worth using for its historical value. The older lady on the right is probably Mrs Ranford with her daughter Mrs Smith on the left. The two children are Albert Smith and his sister, father and aunt of Martin Smith who provided this picture

glover Edward Caney. Beyond was the Worcester Brewery, founded by the Stallard family, and the Worcester Mineral Water Company of Mr D. Shaw, later apparently taken over by the brewery.

The cottages on the corner of Little London were occupied by William Powell, a greengrocer, and Henry John Brown, a glover, and what was later to become Sanders cycle shop, next door to The Talbot, was occupied by John Bourne, a builder and coffin maker.

Further down, on the corner of Somers Road, was the Barbourne Bakery owned by John Morris, possibly the businessman of that name, a plumber by trade, who also ran The Feathers pub at 44 - 45 the Tything.

On the north corner was Edwin Ranford's greengrocers, well known for many years as Teddy Ranford's, specialising in rabbits, then a popular low-cost meat. Martin Smith, whose parents had taken over the shop by 1910, recalls hearing many stories of Teddy Ranford's.

Strings of rabbits sometimes hung outside the shop and locals said: "If you

Ads from St George's parish magazine. Courtesy of Ian Pattison.

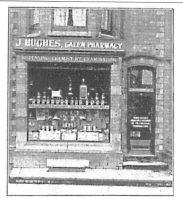

want a rabbit go to Teddy Ranford's." Across the road at No. 1 Brook Villas was a glover named William Ranford, perhaps a relative.

In 1892 John Green, a former gardener at Hawford House near the Kidderminster Road, founded a fruiterer and florist's in distinctive premises which he had built on the corner opposite the end of Paradise Row, where there is now a laundrette. He named the building Covent Garden House, presumably in honour of the great London fruit and veg market.

Mr Green had three daughters, May, Edith and Bertha, the last of whom became involved in helping him run the business which was to continue for half a century or more.

Around this time, opposite Spreckley's Brewery towards the corner of Shrubbery Avenue, was the Hygienic Steam Bakery of T. Fox, specialising in fancy bread and cakes.

On the north corner of Sharman Road from 1896 was the Galen Pharmacy, owned by Mr J. Hughes who must have lived above the premises since in 1903 there was a night bell with which to summon the pharmacist to dispense emergency prescriptions. Mr Hughes also sold toiletries, perfumes and photographic items, much as many chemists' shops do today, and particularly prided himself on his own remedies, "scientifically compounded from the purest ingredients", for treatment of neu-

A 1907 advertisement for the Galen Pharmacy of chemist Mr. J. Hughes.

Covent Garden House on Barbourne Road beyond Paradise Row, now a laundrette. It was built in 1892 by greengrocer and fruiterer John Green; this picture was taken a few years later. The gates on the right, and the garden to which they led, have gone but the plaque on the front of the building, recording the name and date of construction, still remains. Courtesy of Mr Green's great-grandson Ian Pattison.

ralgia, colds, influenza and corns.

In 1898 there were three shops in Barbourne Walk, either just past Pitchcroft Lane where houses now stand, or most probably opposite, where there are still shops. They were Edward Archer's butcher's shop, and the shops of Eliza Bowen and John Halford, though there is no record of what they sold.

There were also evidently some local corner shops dotted around the area. In 1888 baker Edward Eastbury took a five year lease on a shop with accommodation at the corner of Waterworks Road and Pope Iron Road which was not only a bakery but a general store. The lease cost him £24 a year, excluding rates.

In 1902 chocaholics no doubt beseiged the corner of Shrubbery Avenue because it was then that Mr J.A. Whittall opened The Barbourne House Confectionery for sweet and chocolate lovers of every description. In the windows of his shop were mouth-watering rows of glass jars full of sweets of every kind, and on his well-stocked shelves were arranged the products of every English chocolate maker - Cadbury, Fry, Rowntree and Terry's of York - as well as Peter's Swiss Milk chocolate and a tempting array of the choicest French 'confisures'. Mr Whittall's maxim, "No cheap stuff, the best and purest only", lacked something in literary style, but no doubt his customers felt that the quality of the products more than made up for that.

Shopping in Barbourne: 1920s - 1930s

By the 1920s and 1930s it is possible to augment the details from records with the memories of residents, and we are indebted to former and present residents of the area including Mrs Millie Kilbane (nee Hencher), Mrs Gladys Green (nee Meadows), Miss Freda Hibbs, Miss Bridget Monahan, Mr Ron Shuard, Mr Michael Carter, Mr Henry Badham, Mr Martin Smith, Mr Ian Pattison and others, for their invaluable memories of the shops and businesses in Barbourne. Their memories recall a time when there were few cars and no supermarkets; a time when shops specialised in the goods they sold, when shopping was mainly local and going to the shops, even as close by as Barbourne Road, was a big event for youngsters.

Barbourne Road (Hebb Street to the brewery)

Richardsons' Stores were still thriving on the corner of Hebb Street and Millie Kilbane remembers being sent as a youngster from her home in Cumberland Street to fetch a penny packet of tea from Richardsons' or half a pound of carbolic soap, price 2d., for her mother to do the washing. On the opposite corner, where a fish and chip shop now stands, was Harry Hughes' bakery. It had been in business since 1915 or before and was there for many years, though Mr Hughes

Ads from St George's parish magazine. Courtesy of Ian Pattison.

may have gone to fight in the Great War since one older resident recalls he had lost a leg in the war.

Next door to Richardsons' was a chemist's shop, owned for many years by Thomas Lunn who had a shop in the Upper Tything around 1890. In 1903 it was said that, "with one exception", Mr Lunn was the oldest practising pharmacist in Worcester, having been practising for more than 25 years.

The shop's shelves were stocked with items similar to those found in most chemists' shops today - toiletries, perfumes, patent medicines and so on - and like many chemists at that date, Mr Lunn mixed up his own "proprietary remedies" for minor ailments. Later it was Austin Smith's chemists' shop and is now an antique shop.

Next door by the early 1920s was Till's the butchers and Millie Kilbane remembers being sent there for cheap sausage for her granny. There was evidently good money in cheap sausage since butcher Charlie Till also had another shop in The Shambles and lived in one of the large Georgian houses in Paradise Row.

Next door was Strawson's draper's shop where Freda Hibbs recalls you could buy a pair of well boned corsets for 1s 11d (about 10p). Henry Badham recalls that in those far off days of long vanished coinage, Strawson's would give you a packet of pins instead of a farthing if they were short of change.

Next door was the post office, run by the two Miss Hunters and their brother, who continued, like their predecessor from the 1880s, to sell confectionery as well; a business they carried on at No. 9 even after Edgar Cook's grocery store next door was taken over in the 1920s by the Taylors who also took on the post office business.

Thereafter the Paradise Place post office remained at No. 11 until it sadly closed in 2004. It had continued in business for at least one hundred and twenty years and people living in the area might well feel it is hardly progress when Victorian residents had their own post office and modern day residents do not.

By the early 1920s a former butcher's shop owned by George Smith had been taken over by Joe Thorpe the fishmonger with Griffiths, formerly Matthews, the

William Glover's Jersey Dairy in Barbourne, about 1900. The Glover children - Florence, Alfred and Reginald - are standing in the doorway. Courtesy of Jean Glover.

paper

An advertisement for Spreckley's brewery. The Jersey Dairy can just be seen on the extreme left of the picture.

shop next door and Thomas Banning's fruit shop beyond.

At the end of this row of shops was an alleyway, which is still there, running past a row of tall, terraced cottages and connecting with Brewery Walk. Today the alleyway is blocked with a gate at the rear. The only name ever recorded for this small thoroughfare was 'No. 1 Court', shown in an old street directory, and there seems never to have been a sign to that effect.

Beyond the shops, on a site next to Kwik Fit, was the Jersey Dairy at No. 19 Barbourne Road, operated for many years by William Glover. Mr Glover was a native of Bristol who apparently first came to Worcester in 1887, soon after he wed wife Jane, to work as a china decorator at the city's porcelain works. At some time in the next eight years he opened the dairy in premises rented from Spreckley's Brewery, and also set up a butcher's shop in Lowesmoor.

In 1895 the family returned to Bristol and opened a shop there, but they may have retained the butcher's in Lowesmoor, since they moved back there in 1902 and reopened the Jersey Dairy in the following year. The dairy provided the area with fresh milk and a range of produce such as eggs, butter and cheese, as well as dressed poultry, all delivered around the area with a horse-drawn delivery vehicle.

The family subsequently purchased No. 5 St George's Square and stabled the horse there, though the house was let off. Mr Glover had planned to retire to the square but sadly, after 23 years of running the dairy, he died there suddenly in 1927, leaving a widow, two sons and two daughters. The business was taken over by H.T. Bonner & Son and the Glover family moved to the house in St George's Square, which they owned until 1995. William Glover's elder daughter Florence married a Mr Edward Arthur Hibbs of Doncaster and their daughter Freda later taught for 15 years at St Stephen's School. We are grateful to Freda Hibbs and Jean Glover for information on the family.

Beyond the dairy were the buildings of the brewery, by then long since taken over from the Stallard family by the Spreckley brothers and known ever after as Spreckley's Brewery, although it was officially the Worcester Brewery. All that remains today of the brewery buildings on Barbourne Road is a half-circular building, a remarkable bricklaying feat, which was apparently once an engine house to pump water up to the brewery, but is remembered by Mrs Gladys Green of York Place as the 'pop shop' where her brother worked bottling pop in bottles sealed with a marble secured with a clip fastener. She recalls going round as a child in the 1920s picking up a rich booty of marbles which had been dropped by the bottling workers.

Other parts of the brewery, further back from the road, have been saved by incorporation into a housing development. Henry Badham, who grew up in Ashcroft Road, vividly recalls the delivery drays leaving the brewery, pulled by magnificent shire horses. Apparently the draymen were given a stone jar of ale, perhaps because lugging the heavy casks about manually was thirsty work, and since most of the pubs would have given them free drinks also, it's probably just as well that the horses were in charge of the dray! The brewery also had smaller horse-drawn drays for crate deliveries.

Hebb Street area

Off the main road in Hebb Street, on the corner of Ashcroft Road where Lee Design is now based, was Blundell's general store which was certainly open by 1908 and probably earlier. In the early years of the twentieth century it was run by Mrs Emily Blundell and her husband, but by the late 1920s the shop had passed to their daughter Vera, who ran it for many years, at least until the 1950s and possibly longer.

It was there that Henry Badham, retired Head of the Personnel Department at Worcester City Council, who grew up in Ashcroft Road, had his first job as a part-time errand boy. He recalls having to ride on a big old bike to the ice works in Bank Street and struggle back with a large block of ice which Miss Blundell used to make ice cream that Henry then delivered around the area to customers who

Blundell's store on the corner of Ashcroft Road, probably pictured around 1900, with Mrs Emily Blundell and her husband at the shop door and one of Henry Badham's predecessors as errand boy around the corner in Hebb St. Courtesy of Linda from Lee Design.

had ordered it. Henry also recalls that when he began his first 'proper' job as an office boy at the Guildhall he was required to wear full 'civil servant' morning

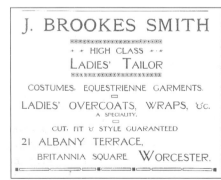

A 1922 advertisement

attire of black jacket, pin-stripe trousers, spats, bowler hat and rolled umbrella! Opposite Blundell's shop, on the other corner of Ashcroft Road, was a fruit and veg and flower shop remembered by both Gladys Green and Henry Badham in the 1920s as Bacon's. Mrs Molly Bacon ran the shop while her son had a lorry which he parked nearby, with which he did some haulage work. The shop was listed as being run by James Bacon in 1922 and Mrs Louisa Bacon in 1937.

A little further west at 21 Albany Terrace was J. Brookes Smith, a "high class" ladies' tailor, specialising in overcoats, wraps and "Equestrienne garments"; it is not clear where exactly this business was because there is no No. 21 since renumbering around 1950.

There were many small tradesmen around the area, invariably working from home, but one of the most successful, at least to judge by his address, was plumber Ralph Ashfield, who lived at Southend, Britannia Square. Mr Ashfield was clearly perceptive enough to note the spread of sewers into the new suburbs and he decided to get into drains, so to speak. Earning himself a certificate from

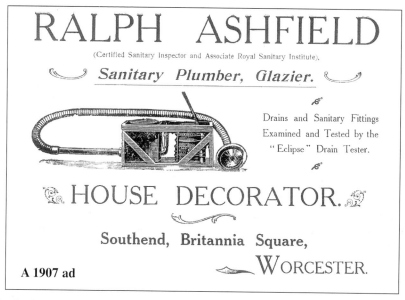

RALPH ASHFIELD
(Certified Sanitary Inspector and Associate Royal Sanitary Institute),

Sanitary Plumber, Glazier.

Drains and Sanitary Fittings Examined and Tested by the " Eclipse " Drain Tester.

HOUSE DECORATOR.

Southend, Britannia Square,

A 1907 ad

WORCESTER.

the Sanitary Institute of London in 1893, he became the local specialist in this type of work, proudly displaying in his adverts a curious looking device called the 'Eclipse Drain Tester', which was said to be the only one of its kind in the city.

Little London area

On the other side of Barbourne Road, shops and businesses had spread along Little London between the homes. The old cottages have long since gone but in the early years of the twentieth century there was a thriving small community here.

The cottages stretching back from the main road on the north side were known as Talbot Row and the first of these was for many years Perrins fried fish shop where those on a tight household budget could get fish pieces for 2d. back in the

1920s. The shop was later owned by Bill Lewis who lived with his wife Rosie in Bromwich Road and had other shops in Bridge Street and Diglis as well as in London.

In 1954 the Jerrum family came from London to manage the Little London shop and son Michael, who now has a butcher's shop at the other end of Barbourne Road, recalls that they got to know the local coppers pretty well because there was a police box opposite where they had to check in every couple of hours.

Next door was Alfred Foxall's sweet shop and, two doors down, a cycle repairer's. In the next cottage hairdresser Chris Hetherington plied his trade from at least 1910 until the early 1920s when he moved to larger premises at 42 Upper Tything and the cycle shop expanded into his premises as well. It was then the Little London Cycle Co. but by 1930 it was trading as Thomas Brown. The Hetherington brothers also later had a couple of branches further along Barbourne Road. Two doors further down was boot repairer George Tetstall and beyond him tailor Ernest Jauncey and greengrocer William Emms.

On the bend, where the road curves round to White Ladies Close, George Gould had been in business for many years as a coachmaker and wheelwright but by the early 1920s the site had turned over to motor repairs and by 1930 it had been taken over by Barbourne Road cycle dealer Fred Sanders as the motor side of the business expanded. Later there was a Christian Science reading room further along.

Opposite, on a site now occupied by the grammar school design block, was the County Garage and above it was The Kings Hall, a popular local dance school and entertainment venue. Beyond the main shopping areas there were many small local corner shops, now sadly gone: Millie Kilbane fondly recalls Granny White's shop in Cumberland Street.

Barbourne Road (Little London to St George's Lane North)

The cottage on the corner of Little London is remembered by many war-time residents of Barbourne as Fred Shuard's butcher's shop. Fred, uncle of Worcester historian Ron Shuard, had emigrated to Australia before the war with his wife Rose, who was formerly 'in service' at Lindisfarne in Barbourne Terrace, the home of the Gascoyne family of hop and seed merchants.

Fred and Rose returned to England when war broke out to make sure that the family were OK, and for the duration of the war Fred took what had long been a butcher's shop on the corner of Little London, formerly Bullocks, and Dan Davies's butcher's shop back in 1910. Ron tells us that his uncle Fred was one of only five butchers in Worcester licensed to slaughter animals; work that was done at the slaughterhouse near the Infirmary, not at his shop. Butcher Jack Williams later had the shop.

Fred and Rose Shuard at their butcher's shop on the corner of Little London. Courtesy of Ron Shuard.

Next door for many years was James Cartwright, the hairdresser. Beyond, in premises now occupied by a sandwich shop, was Fred Sanders' cycle shop, which opened early in 1893 and traded there for many years. At a time when there were many more bikes on the road, and more cycle shops in business, Sanders had a prime position, sold many leading makes and expanded from an early stage with motor repairs.

By this date John Green's fruit and flower business at Covent Garden House had long since become Mapp's greengrocers after Bertha Green, who

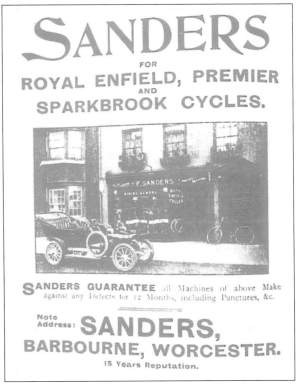

A 1908 advertisement for Sanders cycles next door to The Talbot in Barbourne Road. Courtesy of Clive Haynes, who notes that Sanders had a bicycle riding school and was one of 12 cycle shops in the city then.

was helping her father run the business, met Walter Mapp, who was helping his father run a greengrocer's shop in Pump Street, and they married and took over the Barbourne business, living around the corner in Shrubbery Avenue with Bertha's parents.

Walter had formidable gardening skills, raising grapes in the conservatory and growing a range of produce in the garden at the rear of the shop which has since been built over. Walter and Bertha not only traded from their shop, they also supplied the big houses around the area by bicycle. The shop had an excellent mosaic floor with its trading name, W.H. Mapp, incorporated in the design but this was sadly destroyed some time after the Mapps gave up the business around WWII.

When he was not busy at the shop, Walter had a fine tenor voice and was well-known for his participation in choral works at the Three Choirs Festival, and in

Walter Mapp

Courtesy of Jean Glover

productions of the Worcestershire Operatic and Dramatic Society, for which his brother Thomas, a Droitwich schoolmaster, was a conductor.

He was also choirmaster at Huntingdon Hall where there is still a memorial to his father Thomas, who was Sunday School superintendent there for more than a quarter of a century. We are grateful for this information to Ian Pattison, a descendant of the Greens and Mapps.

Next door to Mapp's was the Lee brothers' Barbourne Hygienic Bakery and tea rooms, which had been in business there since at least 1910. By the early 1920s they had changed the name to St George's Bakery. A sign hung outside and the marks where it was fixed to the wall can still be seen.

Nellie Kilbane recalls that Granny Lee sold off 'day old' cakes to the kids two for a penny and rock cakes two for a halfpenny. She adds: "That was the penny or halfpenny dad gave us for church on a Sunday. We used to keep it and put it in our shoe to buy cakes on Monday. You didn't get much to eat in those days". The Lee brothers had their own cricket team and a ground on the northern outskirts of the city with a pavilion which bore their name.

Beyond the bakery was the long-established butcher's shop of Eastman Ltd. who had another equally long-established branch at No. 60 The Tything not far from Castle Street. Next door was Arthur Keeling the furniture dealer and at No. 30, immediately before Shrubbery Avenue, was The Dorothy Cafe run by the Misses Martin and Godsall, most likely occupying the premises of the Hygienic Steam Bakery of the 1890s.

Just beyond St George's Square, in what is now a cycle shop, was the piano showroom and warehouse of Murdoch & Murdoch and beyond that, on the south side of St George's Lane, was Bailey and Turner's car dealership and garage, previously Onslow's Premier Garage, with hand-cranked petrol pumps outside. The partners also owned an indoor bowling green at the rear of Spreckley's Brewery and Vernon Turner was a well-known

---

LEE BROTHERS,

High Class Bakers. . . .
Confectioners and Caterers.

(The secret of our success in every loaf).

BARBOURNE HYGIENIC BAKERY,
WORCESTER.

A 1910 advertisement

155.

Lee Brothers bakery, now a hairdressers', pictured some time in the Edwardian era to judge by the dress of the unnamed gent in the photograph. Courtesy of Ron Shuard.

local bowler.

He was also an enterprising businessman, making a profit from storage on many sites around the area and owning Barneshall Garage, as well as a stake in Worcester Woodcraft which operated on the bowling green site after the bowling was moved to Orchard Street. Bailey and Turner expanded into haulage at their garage site but the premises were gutted by fire in the 1940s. Above their garage was the Stylish Glove Company and Millie Kilbane recalls them having a show window on the corner of the lane.

Barbourne Road (St George's Lane North to The Swan)

The Co-op on the corner of St George's Lane had not only expanded the former Bond's store but had converted the upper floor to the Co-op hall where Mothers' Union meetings and dances were held. Later there was a youth club for a while.

Beyond the Co-op was Thomas Round's bakery and on the north corner of Brook Street was the hairdressing salon of Fred Homer, a bald-headed barber with a ginger beard, who also opened a tobacconist's shop next door and had a couple of adjoining cottages between his shops and the Swan Inn which were let to other businesses, including boot maker Edward Tyler, general dealer Chris French and butcher Richard Davies. The small row of cottages which constituted Fred's modest business and property empire were known as Swan Terrace. They have been replaced in modern times with a housing development.

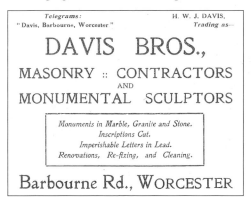

A 1922 advertisement

On the opposite corner of Brook Street, where a furniture store now stands, was Lucy Morris's grocery shop, a family business going back to at least 1910, with Mrs Ann Wood, costumier next door and Davis Brothers, monumental masons, beyond. The area between Davis's and Round's bakery was still entirely residential as late as 1930, but is today entirely occupied by businesses.

Barbourne Road (Barbourne Terrace to Somers Road)

On the north corner of Barbourne Terrace was the old-established business of watchmaker John Burbridge, with Ben Potter's butcher's shop next door and greengrocer George Read, boot repairer Joseph Smith and Reg Brant's tobacconist's shop beyond.

On the south corner of Sharman Road, where there is now a lettings agency, was the high class ladies' wear shop of William Le Bon, who lived around the corner at No. 3 Barbourne Terrace and was said to be a stalwart of the Worcestershire Operatic and Dramatic Society. Another Le Bon, Thomas, presumably a relative, had a tobacconist and newsagent's at 53 The Tything, next to the former Newman's passage, until the early 1920s.

On the opposite corner of Sharman Road for many years was the Galen Pharmacy, fornerly owned by Mr J. Hughes but owned from at least 1915 by Donald Pout who was also the Secretary of the Worcester City and County Pharmacists' Association. He was remembered as always being meticulously dressed right down to his spats, and Martin Smith recalls that whatever you bought, Mr Pout would wrap it carefully with spotlessly white paper and seal it

The Smith family outside A.G. Smith's stores on the corner of Somers Road about 1938. Albert Smith is fourth from left with wife Iris on his left. Courtesy of Martin Smith.

George Smith and his son Albert George, pictured in Somers Road in the 1920s, ran the family haulage business for many years from a yard at the rear of Smith's Stores on the corner of Somers Road. Courtesy of Martin Smith.

with sealing wax. When Mr Pout died, his widow Ruth married a butcher and the pharmacy became a butcher's shop and remains so today, though in different hands.

Next door was a grocer's shop followed by a newsagent's and a draper's, all of which passed through various hands between the war and the 1930s; in 1930 Joseph Burton & Sons had the grocer's, Mrs Dorothy White the paper shop and Miss Isabella Whitehouse the draper's.

On the south corner of Somers Road, John Morris's Barbourne Bakery, which had been in existence from 1884 or before, continued under his control for almost 40 years but had passed to his daughters by the early 1920s and by 1930 it had become Benton's Bakery.

On the opposite corner, where there is now a drycleaner's, Teddy Ranford's greengrocer's had passed down through marriage after his daughter married haulier George Smith. By 1910 George's son, Albert George, had married and taken over the shop which traded for many years as A.G. Smith. It was very much a family affair with Mrs Iris Smith running the shop while husband Albert, following in his dad's footsteps, operated a haulage business from the yard behind where he parked his lorry. We are grateful to Martin Smith for information on the family.

Barbourne Motor Works,
PITCHCROFT LANE.

WIGGALL & BINNALL,
Motor Body Builders,
Coach Builders and Wheelwrights.

ALL KINDS OF SECOND-HAND MOTOR BODIES IN STOCK
LORRY AND FLOAT BUILDERS.

Pitchcroft Lane

Further west in Pitchcroft Lane was the Barbourne Motor Works of Wiggall & Binnall, whose 1922 advertisement is above. They were coach builders and wheelwrights but they had also expanded into motor body as well as lorry and float building and claimed to have "all kinds of second-hand motor bodies in stock".

Barbourne Road (Somers Road to Gheluvelt Park)

Between Somers Road and the park, where there is now a continuous line of shops, there were scarcely any in the early years of the twentieth century and the Victorian villas, like most along Barbourne Road before they became shops, had names as well as numbers.

Gradually a few shops began appearing between the family homes. By 1910 Mrs Mary Brown had opened a 'fancy repository' at Brookfield Villa on the corner of Barbourne Lane, which has recently been rebuilt as an electrical appliance store. By 1922 there was Frank Wilks' ladies and gents' tailors shop at No. 65 where there is now a florist, and on the corner of Barbourne Lane was Mrs Went's sweet shop. The pace of commercial development was slow however and it was some years before the area became as developed as it is today. In what was perhaps a sign of things to come, Griffiths antique shop opened on the corner of Barbourne Lane after the war.

Leisure & Pleasure

Gardens

In the early centuries of the re-born northern suburb the fashionable residents would most likely have gone out of Barbourne to take their leisure, either in the city or at the Saracens Head pleasure ground, behind the pub which still exists at the head of the Tything, where there were pleasant walks and a bowling green accounted the best in the city.

To the west of the Tything was Dr Wall's Walk, presumably established by the Worcester Porcelain founder who was said to have built a house on Foregate Street in front of the Green Dragon; it ran through a cherry orchard to Love's Grove and on to the Pound Fields, on one of which York Place was later built.

There was also a pleasant public walk in the park of Charles Trubshaw-Withers in Samsome Fields in the eighteenth century and this ground was later granted to the city and pleasure grounds established there in 1859 by the Pleasure Garden Company. Amenities included a cricket ground, a bowling green, an arboretum of American conifers, a fountain modelled on one at Witley Court and several flower gardens, but the project was not successful and nine years later the land was sold for housing.

There were pleasant gardens and walks in Barbourne, around The Shrubbery and Barbourne House, but these were private. In the 1880s, according to Worcester historian Bill Gwilliam, the area around the water tanks at the water works was laid out as gardens which were opened to the public for a while.

It was not until Gheluvelt Park opened in 1922 that the area had its own park, though there were public entertainments in the field behind The Talbot and there was always Pitchcroft and the river.

Early Pursuits

Then as now there were circuses and fairs and often also military displays on Pitchcroft, but there were also less laudable displays, such as bull baiting. The year 1816 saw one of the last displays of this kind which was condemned in the press after the bull was "barbarously mangled". The brutal 'sport' of cock fighting was sadly always popular with all ranks of society and Barbourne Lodge had a cockpit in the early eighteenth century at which county teams competed. These tournaments lasted for hours, with frenzied betting on the contests. There were even cock fights between races at race meetings on Pitchcroft.

The Severn watermen had their own barbaric 'sport', recalled by the former Dog and Duck pub opposite Pitchcroft, in which a duck's wing tendons were cut so that it couldn't fly and dogs were then set upon the terrified bird with betting on which one would catch it.

Events

Over the centuries Pitchcroft was often the scene of events of all kinds which drew a wide audience from the area and often from much further afield. In the early nineteenth century it was frequently the scene of bare knuckle bouts, the most famous of which was in 1824 and must rate as one of the most remarkable events Pitchcroft ever saw.

It was a contest between Irish and English champions Jack Langan and Tom Spring for the Championship of All England, and it was so eagerly sought by other venues that it was a miracle it took place here at all. Birmingham and Lichfield both bid strongly for the bout and Warwick offered the fighters £150 each but the fight was secured for Pitchcroft when the Worcester Amateurs put up 300 sovereigns (£315) for each man.

In front of the ageing grandstand, which dated from 1781 or 2, was erected an additional stand for up to 6,000 people and two additional wings were added to cope with the massive numbers of spectators expected to attend.

Tom Spring - Courtesy of Herefordshire Council

The organisers were not disappointed. Every inn and hotel was packed and on the day - 7 January - people arrived from all over England and

162.

The Spring *v.* Langan bare-knuckle boxing match on Pitchcroft in 1824. Courtesy of the Worcester News.

a large contingent of Langan supporters made the long journey from Ireland. Barbourne, along with the rest of Worcester, was packed out with visitors. Inns sold out of refreshments and the carriages of the gentry caused a major parking problem.

By 10am tickets for the fight, which cost a not inconsiderable 10s (50p), had sold out and people scrambled for any vantage point they could find. Sailing ships moored then alongside Pitchcroft and sailors clung precariously to the tops of masts to get a view of the fight. Some commentators estimated the crowd at 30,000, others said 40,000. How many were watching from trees, ships' masts and other such vantage points was never recorded.

Herefordshire-born English champion Tom Spring, real name Thomas Winter, who later became landlord of the Booth Hall pub in Hereford, arrived at 12.30pm in a post chaise to a tremendous cheer from the crowd as he tossed his hat into the ring. Amazingly, no exact time had been fixed for the start of the contest and Spring and the crowd then had to wait an hour for Langan to arrive.

Berrow's Journal claimed to have hired a leading Fleet Street reporter specially for the event and his first comment was on the state of the ground, which had been flooded shortly before. He noted that on the morning of the fight Pitchcroft was so muddy it could not have been cleared in a week "and outside of the ring was nearly a complete sheet of water".

Whether the mud weakened the supports of the temporary stands is not clear, but soon after Spring's arrival, part of the gallery in front of the grandstand, reportedly containing 1,500 people, collapsed hurling screaming, terrified spectators to the ground below.

Berrow's Journal reports of the time suggested that several people were killed as a result and hundreds had to be taken to the Infirmary with broken bones, but Worcester historian David Whitehead claimed in 1976 that the actual number of casualties was just 16. Apparently another gallery containing 2,000 people collapsed soon after the fight started but there were no reports of casualties.

It must have been approaching 2pm when the fight finally got under way and spectators agreed that Spring looked much the larger and tougher of the two and odds lengthened to three to one on Langan.

Despite this, the Irishman had Spring down in the first round and four rounds later the Englishman badly injured, probably broke, his left hand landing a punch on Langan's forehead. But in time Spring's size and weight told and the 24-year-old Langan was eventually blind and barely conscious, despite which he insisted he would go on for another forty rounds! Thankfully the umpire, Colonel Berkeley, didn't agree and declared Spring the winner.

The fight was so exciting that no-one could seem to keep count of anything. Spring was the victor after either 77 rounds or 84, which lasted either two hours and twenty-three minutes or two hours and thirty-nine minutes, depending perhaps on which newspaper you read.

Such events were licensed by the local magistrates and they were subsequently given a severe dressing down by the assize justices for allowing an event to go ahead which posed such threats to public safety.

Events of a very different sort were held on Pitchcroft to celebrate Queen Victoria's great jubilees in the late nineteenth century - a review was staged for the Golden Jubilee in 1887 and further celebrations for the Diamond Jubilee in 1897 - and yet more celebrations, including a parachute descent, were held in June 1902 to mark the coronation of Edward VII.

There were also circuses and fairs. Barnum and Bailey were on Pitchcroft in 1899 and again in 1903 and Pat Collins' fair brought to Worcester a colourful character styling himself 'Sequah, Prince of Quacks', who sold patent medicines and pulled teeth dressed as a Sioux indian chief, surrounded by suitably dressed 'braves' and to the accompaniment of a brass band, which drowned out the screams of his 'patients'.

Horse Racing

Pitchcroft has long been associated with horse racing.. The earliest record of a race meeting there was in 1718, and in the early days there were also foot races, in which men ran around the croft for a prize of a pair of silver buckles and women ran the length of it to win "a handsome hat".

Historians are divided over whether racing then was over natural obstacles, such as hedges around the site, or 'on the flat', but certainly there were no stands for spectators in those early days. Gradually temporary booths began to be erected, probably by landlords of local inns, on top of which spectators could sit, or at least perch precariously, to watch races. The earliest permanent grandstand was erected before 1781-2 and at some stage an inn was built adjacent to the grandstand.

Race meetings were not frequent. As late as 1837 there were still only two meetings a year; one over two days in August and another in November, though these were said to be "well attended and visited by much fashionable company". These meetings were magnets for the country gentry and were accompanied by many social events.

On race days public breakfasts would be held on the bowling greens and in the Portobello Gardens on Henwick Hill, and in the evenings there would be balls and assemblies and packed theatre performances.

By the early nineteenth century racing was being organised by an assemblage of local gentlemen who formed the Worcester Race Committee. The early grandstand was perhaps showing its age by 1823, for in that year the committee sought subscribers for £50 shares to rebuild the stand. Investors were clearly not keen to come forward and six years later they were still trying to raise the money, though they succeeded eventually. The grandstand was rebuilt again about 1901, but by 1929 the Jockey Club was threatening to revoke the course licence and a number of improvements had to be made. The present grandstand was built in 1975.

Swimming

Swimming was inevitably a popular pastime with Barbourne residents, with the river so close by, but it was distinctly unpopular with the Victorian city council since few of the male bathers had costumes and inadvertent displays of male nudity could outrage the modesty of passing ladies.

The city council's solution was a sunken bathing 'barge', an oblong floating wood and wire mesh cage moored at the river bank, which allowed the water to flow through. The first barge was sited at the top of Pitchcroft in 1879, perhaps to keep the bathers out of female sight, since it was not accompanied by changing facilities. In 1895 plans were made to replace this with a new, larger barge.

Ladies, meanwhile, continued to be outraged, mainly by the fact that there were no facilities for them. Councillors were petitioned ro retain the old barge for the use of ladies, but as soon as they agreed it promptly sank! The council bowed to the inevitable and stumped up for two new bathing barges, which were situated just south of the racecourse grandstand in 1896. They are remembered by users as providing a relatively safe, if somewhat murky, environment for swimmers. By 1928, and probably before, there were changing cubicles on the bank.

The inflexible rule of the swimming barges was to keep to your own barge - absolutely no mixed bathing allowed - and the council engaged an attendant to ensure this rule was kept at all times. Around the turn of the century the swimming barge attendant was a local man named Charles Webb who sported a magnificent growth of beard. Apparently another of his official duties as attendant was to recover the bodies of people drowned in the Severn.

For those with greater means, there was a private hotel not too far away which offered an altogether more exotic experience. The open-air baths in Sansome Walk, on the site of the present swimming baths, were built and opened in 1854 by a Mr Barber from Chelterham.

The long two-storey building had an entrance porch impressively supported by stone caryatids, said to have been left over from a building project in Cheltenham. The baths passed to the Lett family in the 1860s and then in 1878 to Charles Bartholomew.

Their appeal was initially through a plethora of 'spa' style baths, including sulphur, iodene, salt and calomel, as well as Bartholomew's own 'nature cure'.

As these fell out of favour the Turkish baths became the most popular.

From 1890 William Park managed and subsequently owned the business for 56 years. He was said to be one of the greatest authorities in the country on Turkish and other bath treatments and was also well-known in Worcester as a JP and a fund raiser for the infirmary. He died aged 91 in 1955. After his retirement, management of Park's Baths passed to his son Leonard, and it continued to have the only public swimming pool in the area. It was replaced by the present municipal indoor baths in 1972.

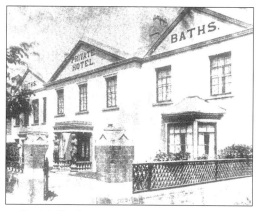

Park's Baths - courtesy of Clive Haynes

In 1900 the council had passed a bye-law forbidding river bathing anywhere but at the barges, but there was no chance of that being observed for long, and by the 1920s swimmers were once more bathing in the river from all along Pitchcroft. For those with a need for speed, a swimming race was held in the 1930s from the Kepax ferry to the grandstand.

Most Barbourne youngsters, who could afford neither Park's baths nor the barges, learnt to swim for free in the Severn during summer holidays. Favourite spots included Northwick slip and Sandy Bay, roughly in the centre of Pitchcroft, opposite the Dog and Duck pub from which a ferry ran. It was so called because in those far-off days there really was sand there.

Martin Smith, originally from Somers Road, learnt to swim there. "We all learnt to swim there," recalls Martin. He believes the bow waves, from petrol tankers which then used the river, stirred up sand from the river bed and deposited it on the river margin to create this little bit of inland seaside. There is a natural seam of gravel and sand running under Barbourne which could account for this, but Henry Badham, originally from Ashcroft Road, recalls the council helping the process along by depositing sand there.

The tankers, which took petrol up to Stourport, from where it went by pipeline to Coventry, stopped operating in 1956 and Sandy Bay is now silted up and muddy. Non-swimmers always had to be careful not to paddle out too far because the bottom suddenly dropped away sharply.

The swimming barges had fallen out of use by the early 1970s when the new swimming baths opened in Sansome Walk, and the changing cubicles were demolished in 1975 when work began on the new grandstand.

Cruising

For adults the pleasure was more often in being on the river rather than in it. During the summer months a cruise on the river was, and still is, a popular choice for public trips, private parties and club and works outings, and a number of steamers plied their trade on the Severn. Most passengers embarked at South Parade, but in the past the steamers also stopped at the Waterworks to pick up Barbourne and Northwick passengers.

Holt Fleet was a popular destination for an afternoon cruise but other trips went to Stourport, Kempsey, Pixham Ferry and The Ketch, Upton and Tewkesbury and larger steamers even went as far afield as Gloucester and Sharpness Point.

The largest fleet on the river belonged to the Castle Line which had its offices at the Rectifying House. A familiar sight on the river during the second half of the nineteenth century was the line's steamer The Perseverance, originally a paddle steamer, which was launched from Stevens' Yard near the railway bridge in 1868 and was photographed at Holt Fleet around 1890 packed with so many people that it's a wonder it didn't sink. It was taken out of service in 1904.

By then the line had three other steamers in service; the little 50-passenger Hanley Castle, the Avonmore Castle carrying 230 and the Holt Castle, then the largest steamer on the Severn, with a capacity of 326 passengers. The two larger vessels had "commodious and splendidly-fitted" saloons which could seat up to 60 for lunch or tea.

Their chief rival at the turn of the century was the Duchess of York, later re-named The Duchess Doreen, owned and captained by George Williams, whose father John had founded the business in the mid-nineteenth century. It was teak built, with a capacity of 167 passengers, and was said to be the most valuable boat in the Severn fleet. By the 1920s the vessels Beatrice, Star and Dove were also on the river.

Boating

Many people preferred to cruise the Severn under their own power and all along the river there were rowing boats for hire. John Williams had begun in business hiring pleasure boats from South Parade, and in times past there were at least five other boat hire stations between the road bridge and Barbourne Brook. The Morris family at the bottom of Waterworks Road, have been running one of these since the 1940s. They were preceded there by a Mr Thornborough. Today they are the only ones still keeping up the tradition.

They recall that both Mr Bromwich at the Dog and Duck ferry and Mr Long at the Kepax ferry had boats for hire. Boats were also for hire by the grandstand, near the cathedral from Frank Roberts and later from the Seabornes of Diglis who subsequently moved to Kempsey, and by Tommy Bolch further along the river.

Jacqueline Morris recalls that the Morris family used to make their own boats, first in timber, later in fibreglass, and so did some other boat hirers.

For those who preferred their rowing with a competitive sporting edge the Ariel Boat Club was founded in 1841 and the Worcester Rowing Club in 1875; by 1886 it had a boathouse in the same position as the present one. These clubs were the inheritors of a long tradition of rowing races on the river, which are believed to have been taking place as early as 1790. The first city regatta was held in 1845 with races from Diglis to the Dog and Duck. Part of Pitchcroft was cordoned off for paying customers, booths and stalls were erected and painted barges moored on the river brought a real carnival atmosphere to proceedings.

Pubs

For those who prefer their liquid in a glass there is good news. Unlike many parts of the city which have lost well-known hostelries, Barbourne has retained most of its traditional pubs. There were never many pubs around the Barbourne Road, but for the most part they have stayed open.

The eponymous Barbourne Inn, at 18 New Bank Street, has become The Barbourne, though an etched window still records the original name. The Barbourne was owned originally by Robert Allen's little Barbourne Brewery which was based at 13 - 17 on one side of the pub and had its offices and stores at 19 - 20.

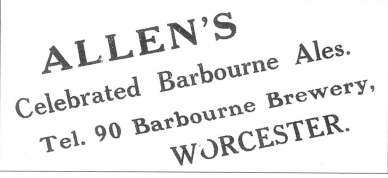

A 1922 ad for Robert Allen's Barbourne Brewery

The Pope Iron, which for a time after its removal from Severnside to Pope Iron Road was the New Pope Iron, has sadly been renamed The Winning Post in recent years. The only actual casualty since the mid-nineteenth century has been the little Royal Oak at 45 - 46 York Place, which closed in the 1960s.

The remaining pubs in Barbourne, which are still with us today, are The Swan, a house of probably very ancient foundation opposite the park, and The Talbot in

169.

Paradise Row which, though not so ancient, has an interesting history. Other popular watering holes in the Upper Tything were the Coach and Horses at No. 39 and The Feathers, formerly The Plume of Feathers, now renamed, at 44 - 45. Also not too far away, and still with us, is the Chesnut Tree in Lansdowne Road. Millie Kilbane, originally from Cumberland Street, recalls that in the 1930s beer was 4d. a pint and a tot of rum was the same, as was a Green Goddess, an horrendous-sounding concoction which contained rum, whiskey, beer and a good deal else!

It wasn't only drinking that went on in the pubs. In the days when off-course betting was illegal, the bookie's runner came to the Coach and Horses to take surreptitious bets and returned later with the cash if you were a winner. But there were three 'coppers' living in the area and one of them, PC Edgar Davies, liked a drink when he was off duty. When he turned up in the Coach and Horses for his pint the bookie's runner had to make himself scarce.

Dancing

For the young and active, then as now, dancing was the thing to do on Friday night. The Co-op hall at St George's Lane held dances, but the most popular venue was at the other end of Barbourne.

The King's Hall, above a garage off Little London, where the Royal Grammar School design block is now situated, was the home in the 1920s of the Central School of Dancing run by Chas and Mabel Haines, a local acrobatic dance team who also organised open-air dances in Cripplegate Park, and whose daughter trained for the ballet and went on to take up dancing professionally.

Henry Badham from Ashcroft Road remembers that the Friday night dances were very popular, perhaps not least because he recalls it was very cheap to get in. There were no DJs in those days of course; music had to be live and was provided by Billy Gammon and his 'Star Players'.

Billy Gammon and the Star Players

Billy Gammon in the 1950s. This picture and that of the Star Players are reproduced courtesy of Mike Grundy and the Worcester News

Billy had been the pianist at Chas and Mabel's open-air dances and also with a six-piece band at the Star Hotel, hence the name he took for his own band. The Players - they called themselves an orchestra for posh engagements - apparently became resident at the Star for a time, but were famed chiefly for their regular engagements in Cheltenham and in Malvern Priory Park and at the Winter Gardens, and in the 1930s they broadcast regularly in a 6.30pm slot from the BBC's studios in Broad Street, Birmingham, but the King's Hall dances must have been one of their first regular engagements.

After the war Billy Gammon gave up music and started a successful engineering firm, Star Engineering in Malvern, which originated the 'push-twist' controls found on most modern gas appliances, but more than twenty years later he was still being referred to in the local press as "perhaps the best-known name in the Midlands dance band world".

Cycling

Some people, of course, preferred clean living and exercise and in that period the chief amongst these were the cycling enthusiasts. The bicycle was then the only available alternative to walking for many people, and by the end of the nineteenth century there were a dozen cycle manufacturers in the city and perhaps as many clubs for leisure cycling, with interests ranging from racing to leisurely Sunday rides.

Barbourne cycling club the 'Gheluvelt Wheelers' started in the 1920s and originally met outside the main gate of the park, but when their numbers grew too large they moved meetings to the scout hut in Somers Road. Henry Badham from Ashcroft Road was a member and recalls that they went on a long trip every Sunday. A friendly farmer even lent them a cottage at Trotshill for use during Sunday rides. The club also held races; Henry won a bronze medal in one. But this weekend fun was strictly for men only - no girls allowed! - and when Henry got a girlfriend and bought a tandem he had to drop out of the club.

Leisure cycling was still going strong in the 1940s and early 1950s. Martin Smith, then from Somers Road, was a member of the Barbourne Monarchs, who

The Barbourne Monarchs cycling club at their speedway track on Pitchcroft in 1952. Pictured, from left, are Joe Hencher, Martin Smith, Graham Bailis, Collen Greenway, Jeff Trow, Ken Chapman, John Wilkes and Roger Smith. Courtesy of Martin Smith.

had their own cycle speedway track on Pitchcroft, and he had the distinction of being the only Individual Cycle Speedway Champion of Worcester ever in 1951. He recalls that as winner he was presented with a small individual cup to keep and a large cup to be handed on from year to year - but since the contest was never held again he got to keep both!

Terrence 'John' Green from York Place was also a formidable competitive cyclist in the early 1950s, though he rode with a St John's club.

He was champion cyclist for three years running, the first in the club to do 25 miles in less than an hour and the winner of an horrific-sounding endurance race

Martin Smith from Somers Road became Worcester's first and only Cycle Speedway Champion, when he won the title in 1951, aged 18. He received a small individual cup to keep and another to be re-awarded annually, but the contest was never run again - so he still has both.

which involved riding from Worcester to Birmingham, down to Weston and back

Barbourne Bowling Club in 1911. Courtesy of Ron Shuard.

to Worcester in under 13 hours.

Bowling

Bowling was always popular in the area and the green at the Saracens Head was the most fashionable in the city in the eighteenth century.

The Barbourne Bowling Green Club, which is still going strong today, was founded in 1897 and incorporated in 1899 with its registered office and green in Redcliffe Street, where the club is still based.

The rules of the club provided that there should be no more than 70 members, all of whom were shareholders. The club was open from 9am to 11.30pm daily from May to October. Members paid an annual subscription but in addition losers had to pay 3 pence to the winner of a game, one penny of which the winner had to pay to the 'games box'.

There was an indoor bowling green near the end of York Place after WWII, set up by Vernon Turner, a well-known local bowler and one half of the Bailey and Turner garage partnership at the end of St George's Lane North, but that green was later removed to Orchard Street.

Football

In the nineteenth century most parishes had their own cricket and football teams. In the early twentieth century two of the best of the local teams were Berwick Rangers from Bath Road and Worcester Rovers, who had no set playing field.

After playing each other for the last time on Pitchcroft in 1904 they amalgamated to form Worcester City Football Club and played for some years on Thorneloe, now a school playing field at the north end of Pitchcroft, before moving to St George's Lane.

In the early days times were hard. In the first year of their amalgamation they were due to play away at Stoke but had no money to finance the fixture. The situation was only retrieved after the players offered to forego their wages and club president Lord Beauchamp had a whip-round to raise the train fare.

Despite these financial problems, which might be familiar to many lower league clubs today, the 'city' had many successes, winning the Birmingham League and beating Aston Villa and West Bromwich Albion reserve teams.

As we write, a century of Worcester City Football Club in Barbourne seems about to come to an end with the proposed move of the club to a new ground south of the city.

Cricket

By 1882 there was a very well organised cricket club in St Stephen's parish, which originally drew its players from the area near St Stephen's School, perhaps former pupils, but which eventually became one of the leading teams in the district and drew its players from a much wider area.

It was originally called Claines Cricket Club, but this was thought misleading and it was soon changed to Barbourne Cricket Club. This name became known throughout the area in subsequent years as one of the two leading clubs in and around Worcester, locked in competition with their arch-rivals, St John's Cricket Club.

Education

Early Days

Barbourne has long had a reputation for the variety and excellence of its educational institutions. The earliest known educational establishment in the area was founded in the 1760s at Barbourne Lodge by Richard Burney, a relative of the novelist Fanny Burney, who taught dancing and music, both vital accomplishments for the sons and daughters of tradesmen and farmers. More information on the Burneys is included in notes on the Lodge.

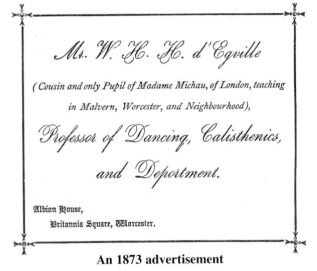

Mr. W. H. H. d'Eqville

(Cousin and only Pupil of Madame Michau, of London, teaching in Malvern, Worcester, and Neighbourhood),

Professor of Dancing, Calisthenics, and Deportment.

Albion House,
Britannia Square, Worcester.

An 1873 advertisement

This was by no means the last dancing school to appear in the area; no doubt the classy addresses gave the right image for this kind of business. There was a Mr Painter, a dancing master, in the Tything in 1790.

In 1873 a Mr W.H.H. d'Eqville operated a similar establishment at Albion House, Britannia Square, styling himself "Professor of Dancing, Calisthenics and Deportment" and claiming to be the "cousin and only pupil of Madame Michau of London", though who that clearly distinguished lady was is not known. Mr d'Eqville's school may have been long established since someone of that name was reported in the local press to be organising a concert in November 1837.

Music also continued to be taught in private schools in the area; in 1884 the splendidly named Arthur Richard Quartermain was based at No. 7 The Tything, styling himself Professor of Music, while Miss Amelia Pullen at No. 17 preferred the more modest title of teacher of music.

Private Education

In the same decade that the Burneys arrived at Barbourne Lodge a Miss Harris founded the first known Barbourne 'school' in the usual sense of the word, at Thorneloe House, establishing a pattern which would be followed over the next couple of centuries by other enterprising, unmarried ladies.

The novels of Jane Austen and Charlotte Bronte make painfully clear just how few options life offered to educated but poor young women in the eighteenth century, and starting a school was much preferable to life as a governess in a wealthy household, offering more independence and, hopefully, a better income.

The Bronte sisters tried to start a school at Haworth, though without success, but Miss Hariss's school at Thorneloe House - covered in more detail in notes on the building - prospered for a quarter of a century or more, and other large houses in the area were to prove as attractive for the purpose of educational establishments, though none could claim the distinction Miss Harris had of counting one of England's greatest actresses amongst her first pupils.

Education statistics, included in Bentley's Directory of 1842, show that Worcester, with a population of 27,000, second in the Worcestershire of that time only to Dudley with 31,000, came only sixth in the league table of day schools for local youngsters, with one school to every 628 people in the city; Redditch had almost double that number per head of population and even small towns like Upton and Stourport were outperforming the county town.

What Worcester did have though was one of the highest incidences of boarding schools in the county, with some 23 schools or one to every 1174 people in the population, and directories and press advertisements suggest that Barbourne had its fair share of these, if not more.

In 1842, prior to Mr d'Eqville's sojourn at Albion House, Britannia Square, a ladies' boarding school was based there, run by (the Misses?) Impey and Westcombe, a boys' school was conducted there by Frederic Marcus and at that same date a Miss H. Belson conducted a ladies' seminary at Baskerville House.

In that same year there were two schools in St George's Square, the gents' boarding academy of F.A. Walters MA at No. 16 and the ladies' boarding school of Haynes and Deering at No. 27.

In the mid-nineteenth century the Simpsons at Thames House ran what was reputedly the principal private school in Worcester. In 1865 a Miss Jenkins offered to receive "a limited number of young ladies to board and educate on modest terms" at 2 Barbourne Terrace. In 1869 there was a boarding Ladies'

EDUCATION.

2, BARBOURNE TERRACE.

MISS JENKINS

RECEIVES A LIMITED NUMBER OF

Young Ladies to Board and Educate

ON MODERATE TERMS.

TERMS AND REFERENCES FORWARDED ON APPLICATION.

Private school advertisements from the 1860s

PRIORY HOUSE ACADEMY,
TYTHING, WORCESTER.

(Established upwards of 20 years.)

J. T. HYDE, Principal.

The especial aim of this School is to prepare Boys for BUSINESS LIFE, the Education being THOROUGHLY COMMERCIAL, and adapted to the requirements of the present age, embodying all that is useful in the methods of the most eminent Educators ; thus enabling the Pupils to engage in COMMERCIAL, ENGINEERING, AGRICULTURAL, and MANUFACTURING pursuits.

The system of Instruction pursued is of the most comprehensive kind, and includes all that is necessary for the development of the Intellectual Faculties.

PROSPECTUSES OF TERMS AND REFERENCES ON APPLICATION PERSONALLY, OR BY POST.

1, BARBOURNE, WORCESTER.

LADIES' SCHOOL,

CONDUCTED BY MISS WOOD,

ASSISTED BY MASTERS AND RESIDENT GOVERNESSES.

In this Establishment Young Ladies receive a sound and accomplished Education, with the privileges and comforts of Home.

TERMS, 25 GUINEAS AND 30 GUINEAS PER ANNUM.   ACCOMPLISHMENTS EXTRA.

Pupils taken for a term of years, without vacations when required.

PREPARATORY SCHOOL

FOR

YOUNG GENTLEMEN.

WHITE LADIES' HOUSE,
TYTHING, WORCESTER.

MRS. ALLGOOD

Undertakes to instruct Young Gentlemen in all the usual branches of Education in such a manner as thoroughly to fit them for their entrance into more advanced Schools, while their moral training, health, and general deportment are carefully attended to.

An 1869 advertisement for a private school

School, conducted by a Miss Wood "assisted by masters and resident governesses", which gave its address as '1 Barbourne' and offered "a sound and accomplished education" on terms of 25 and 30 guineas (£26.25 and £31.50) per annum.

At that date a Mr J.T. Hyde was principal of the Priory House Academy which had been established for more than 20 years in the Tything, offering an education which was said to be "thoroughly commercial...enabling pupils to engage in commercial, engineering, agricultural and manufacturing pursuits".

On a wholly different level, in terms of fees if nothing else, was the Finishing School for Young Ladies, boarders only, at Albany Lodge, Britannia Square, presided over by Miss Cooke. Fees of 40 guineas (£42) a year included, said an 1873 advertisement, "eminent masters and resident English, Foreign and Music Governesses, to educate in all the subjects recquisite for a thorough English Education".

In the early 1880s the Misses Green were running the grandly named Worcester Ladies' College at Thorneloe House, and the Misses Osborn were conducting a ladies' boarding school at Raby House, 6 Albany Terrace, which, according to the Worcester Herald, later removed to Barbourne Terrace and still existed around 1930.

In 1883 one of the area's best-known private boarding schools, Barbourne College, opened on the Barbourne House estate now occupied by Gheluvelt Park, under its formidable principal and owner Mr W.P. Caldwell, who continued as headmaster thoughout the quarter of a century during which the college operated.

Caldwell may have been Irish - certainly he was educated at Trinity College, Dublin, and sent his son there - and many of the college's pupils came from

An 1896 view — Barbourne College. From the grounds

Ireland, though they were also drawn from across the UK and as far afield as South Africa.

The school had preparatory and senior departments, taking boys from the age of six up to what we would now call sixth form. The principal was particularly keen on physical training and every pupil was required to gain a swimming certificate.

The college expanded in 1894 by leasing the nearby Lavender House, and it was well equipped, boasting its own science lab, open air swimming baths with a diving board, gymnasium and cricket, tennis and croquet areas. The main house was set in 18 acres of landscaped grounds which were said to have made it one of the finest school properties in the Midlands.

The college was reportedly flourishing in 1903 but it closed five years later, perhaps on the retirement of the formidable Mr Caldwell, and the house and land were subsequently sold for £3,000.

All of these private schools, and others which came and went over the years, had one thing in common: Barbourne was not their 'catchment area' but simply a convenient location for them, and they sought their pupils, at the very least throughout the area and often throughout the country and beyond.

The boarding schools especially, might be attracting their pupils from far and wide, educating the sons or daughters of minor colonial officials or missionary

The old Pound House in Pound Walk, in use as a gymnasium for Tredennyke House school. Courtesy of Ron Shuard.

clergymen - in fact anyone with a limited budget but a hankering for a supposedly superior boarding education for their offspring, or the need to ship the kids off to school while they ran the empire.

With the opening of the twentieth century came day schools which no doubt catered for local children as well as youngsters from across the city. In 1903 Mrs A.E. Grisman was principal of the Rothsay House School in Britannia Square, which had opened seven years earlier. It was described in a local newspaper as "a very successful school for girls with an equally successful department for little boys, who are thoroughly grounded in English subjects, Latin and French in preparation for grammar schools".

From 1910 or before, Miss M.E. Faulds ran a private preparatory school, College House, at No. 20 Barbourne Road, at the north end of Paradise Row, though by 1930 the school had expanded into No. 18 as well. Ian Pattison, who was a pupil there in the 1940s, recalls that the staff were Miss Hutchinson and Miss Watkiss whom he remembers as "a bit of a tartar".

In the garden was a hut, known as the 'tin tabernacle', a name originally given to a temporary classroom in use at the grammar school from 1895 until 1938. The building with that nickname at College House was used by a Mr Bradley, an upholsterer, and Ian recalls watching him work after school.

Around the same time there was a boys' prep school at Tredennyke House on the corner of Barbourne Crescent and Barbourne Terrace, which used as its gymnasium the old pound house nearby where goods had once been impounded until city tolls were paid. As late as 1902 these tolls and dues were still making the city almost £1600 a year, which may not sound much, but did back then.

Another well-known Barbourne prep school was Sunnyside School, which was founded in 1914 by Muriel Tysoe, who had come to the area from Gloucestershire two years earlier, as governess to the children of a Rev W.L.J. Ford. He was said to have been so impressed by her ability as a teacher that he helped her set up a school at St Stephen's Lodge in Droitwich Road, which started with just six children.

Numbers rose fast and in 1934, with 100 on roll, the school moved to Sunnyside Road. Miss Tysoe continued as head for an amazing 53 years until 1967, but after she retired numbers fell. The school closed at the end of 2005 but the nursery school, first opened in 1973, still continues.

Catholic Education

There were no Catholic schools in Barbourne but Catholic education developed close by and attracted scholars from Barbourne and was, albeit inadvertently, partly responsible for the establishment of the first school in Barbourne for local youngsters, so it is worth mentioning here.

A new Catholic church was opened in Sansome Place in July 1829 and on 29 November of that year worshippers in the city were summoned to a meeting to consider the establishment of a school. A Sunday School was opened with boys and girls taught separately, in two rooms off a yard near the church. A master and mistress were subsequently engaged and a day school opened in rented rooms in Silver Street, which attracted many youngsters from non-Catholic families in Barbourne, desperate to educate their children.

The first purpose-built school, for 'poor' children, was erected about 1834 behind the presbytery in Sansome Place at a cost of £500. It provided two partitioned classrooms, but within 16 years two more were needed.

This expansion may have been the result of the involvement, from 1848, of the Daughters of the Heart of Mary, a religious order which favoured lay dress. Their most notable local member was Miss Caroline Walsh, whose family lived at Lower Wick House.

She founded a 'Middle Class School for Girls' at 11 Britannia Square in the 1850s, which was subsequently attended by Edward Elgar and his sisters Lucy and Pollie. The school closed in the 1860s, but the house remained in control of the order; Miss Walsh died there on 22 July 1878, aged 71.

Members of another religious order, the Sisters of Charity of St Paul, from Selly Park, Birmingham, ran a school in the city from 1876 until 1984, and lived for a time, in the early years of the school, at 10 Britannia Square. A full history of Catholic education in Worcester is included in the history of St George's Catholic Church.

Primary Schools

The earliest school dedicated to the education of local children was founded by Rev. James Tyrwhitt, the first curate of St George's. On his arrival at the chapel in the square, which opened in 1830, he was horrified to find that there was no schooling available for children in the area, especially so since some thirty of his parishioners, desperate to educate their children, had sent them to the catholic school in Sansome Walk.

In an age when religious tolerance was much less in evidence than it is today, Rev. Tyrwhitt talked darkly about "bribes and other means" being used to "enveigle" children into the Catholic school, and he set about providing a school for them in the parish.

One of the still empty house plots, roughly in the centre of the south side of the square, contained an open cowshed owned by the churchwarden, and it was there that he subsequently set up the first St George's parish school, creating two schoolrooms for boys and girls and collecting subscriptions from parishioners to fund a master and mistress.

"The school", he wrote, "is situated in a field near to St George's Chapel, and is well ventilated, with a brick floor, and the ages of the children vary from 5 to 13, but are mostly under 10.

"There are forms or benches for the classes not repeating viva-voce. I am educating 120 comfortably." An educational charity he approached for help was also horrified, since they considered the space he had was suitable for only 18 pupils!

He stayed for perhaps only a year afterwards, but Rev.Tyrwhitt had proved that there was a substantial demand for education in the area, though finding the resources to meet it would not be easy.

By the end of 1833 the building plot on which the cowshed stood had been sold and the school had to be removed. A Mr Laslett offered a site next to the chapel but no funds could be found to build new premises for the school, which was already, according to its first balance sheet, 24 pounds and five shillings in debt.

A new incumbent, the Rev George Cole, took over in 1834 and got the project moving again. A site was selected - the one on which the school still stands in what was then Flag Lane, now St George's Lane North - and an estimate of £354 was obtained for the building of a school with two schoolrooms measuring 40 feet by 20 feet and ten feet high, in which 125 boys and 125 girls could be educated.

St George's School Standard 1 1935. Martin Smith, who provided the picture, has identified older brother Eric Smith, third from right, bottom row, and his friend Roy Burbridge, fourth from left, second row down.

The Treasury came up with £125 and £40 came from the National Society, an educational charity, with, presumably, the parish having to find the rest of the money. The school opened in 1835 and in the following year had 90 boys and 70 girls on roll.

The Rev Cole noted with pride that "the number is continually increasing", but by 1855 there were only 65 boys and 65 girls on roll; John Bishop was then master and Sarah Jane Pritchard mistress, but this modest staffing would have been supplemented by older pupils acting as unpaid teaching assistants to teach the younger children.

In 1862 St George's was one of more than a dozen 'National Schools' in the city. These were the forerunners of today's primary schools but they were not primaries as we know them; they were elementary schools, and in most cases would provide the only education pupils would get, since there was no automatic progression to secondary schooling except for the well-off, and sometimes for the gifted.

The introduction of the 1870 Education Act, which provided public funds for school building, gave rise to a plan for a new school with three schoolrooms to accommodate 350 children, to be partly funded by the sale of the existing school site and buildings, but no buyer could be found and thus St George's has stayed where it is right up to the present day.

Expansion was inevitable however, in a fast-growing area. By 1876 two more classrooms, one for infants, had been added, at which date there were 82 boys, 45 girls and 65 infants on roll.

In 1911 the then vicar of St George's, Rev Canon Isaac, brought about the building of a new infants school and extensive refurbishment of the existing buildings, but these alterations were later judged unsatisfactory and the schools were black-listed by the Board of Education.

Several subsequent vicars were involved in further energetic fund-raising and in 1936 work started on conversion of the buildings into a 'modern' junior school, at an estimated cost of £1,500, though the actual bill came to £3,000. The new buildings were opened on 24 April 1937.

Many former St George's pupils and their parents may recall head Mr L.W. Workman, who took over in September 1953, and his deputy from January 1967, Mr M. Richards, who later succeeded to the headship.

The other school for local youngsters was St Stephen's, opened in 1864 thanks to the generosity of two local ladies, Miss Jane Lavender and her sister Mrs Mary Gutch, who funded the building of both church and school.

In those far-off days education was not compulsory, there was no fixed leaving age and no such thing as free education, though the fees at the new school were said to be "easy".

Within a very few years St Stephen's was being praised by inspectors for its

1897
Mesdames Marks, Cropper, Martin, Barker, Rofe, Whittall, Diaper, Whitehouse, Price and Gegg.

1960
Mrs. Pethord; Mr. Asbury; Mr. Jackman; Mr. Sadler; Mr. Jackson; Miss Walsh; Miss Hill; Mrs. Barrs; Mr. Langley; Miss Hibbs and Mrs. Marsden.

St Stephen's School staff in 1897 and 1960, in the centenary publication

186.

high standards and throughout its existence it regularly won a trophy-cabinet-full of competitive awards and saw many pupils win scholarships to senior schools. The school is sadly no longer in existence but a good deal is known about its history, thanks to a centenary publication produced in 1964.

The school was built by Thomas Wilkes who was actually the local undertaker, at least until 1879 when he died at the early age of just 40, but in his short life he had also branched out into construction, building St Stephen's and Claines schools and many houses in the area.

St Stephen's was intended to cater for 90 boys and 90 girls, but when it opened on 26 September 1864 under the first headmaster, David Freeman, formerly head of Godalming National School, only the boys' schoolroom was ready.

At that time youngsters of all ages were educated together in the one room, the older ones helping the younger. Rows of desks were raised on a series of levels so the teacher could easily see every child from his desk.

The first vicar of St Stephen's church, Rev T.G. Curtler, became a trustee and took a keen interest, making regular visits to the school, talking to parents and pupils and teaching chess to the older children.

Heads then had a great deal of freedom in the way they organised their school, and Freeman's successor was chiefly remembered for long playtimes and afternoon walks in the country.

In 1870 a new, stricter national education regime was introduced and an energetic young head named Craddock was brought in, who was to play a major part in the development of the school. The new head proved that working long hours is not just a modern phenomenon.

He reorganised staffing, appointing as pupil teachers two older boys who later went on to qualify as teachers, and giving them lessons from 7 - 8am. He introduced new classes in science and art, streamed pupils in other subjects to provide education at an appropriate level for all learners and he started evenings classes five nights a week for ex-pupils who needed to further their education.

He drove pupils as hard as he drove himself, and as if all this weren't enough, he also taught on Saturdays at the private school of a Mr Marcus in Castle Street. Two young ladies named Craddock, presumably the head's daughters, later joined the staff as pupil teachers.

As the list of prizes and certificates given at awards events lengthened, the school's reputation grew and parents from far beyond St Stephen's parish began to send their children there. In 1886-7 substantial additions were required to school buildings to cope with the numbers attending, not least because house building was going on apace in the parish.

Mr Craddock kept up his unrelenting pace for more than 30 years, but in 1902 he was ordered to take a complete rest. He retired eight years later at the end of 1910, having seen not only a much greater liberalisation of education as new sub-

St Stephen's Church, courtesy of Jane Booth.
Church and school shown on a map of 1884

jects and methods came in, but also a massive growth in the parish surrounding the school and in the numbers on roll. After all his labours, it is pleasing to record that Mr Craddock enjoyed almost 11 years of retirement before his death in September 1921.

He was succeeded in January 1911 by Mr H. J. Knights who began his own reorganisation of the school along 'modern' lines. There were increased facilities for handicrafts, visits to places of interest, the introduction of class libraries to stimulate reading, PT and swimming joined the timetable and football and cricket in a field off Lavender Road from 1914. But in that year war broke out and the head and several male members of staff joined up, not returning until the spring of 1919, and had to be replaced by temporary staff for the duration. They returned to a county impoverished by the war and producing educational improvements with a lack of resources was slow going.

In 1930 there was an epidemic of measles followed by an outbreak of scarlet fever, disrupting the work of the school for six months. Nevertheless the school continued to obtain glowing reports from inspectors for its teaching - though there was increasing concern about the state of the buildings.

The inadequate heating was hopefully at the top of the inspectors' list. On at least one occasion in 1929 writing lessons could not go ahead because ink had frozen in the ink pots! New coke stoves were introduced, but they made little difference, according to this account by teacher Mr E.C.M. Baker, who joined the staff in September 1931:

> "The cramped conditions under which I found myself teaching 40 boys were most disconcerting for they were taught literally alongside another class of similar number with no partition between us. One light, like a star, shone out over each class. The windows wouldn't budge, which was just as well in winter! One miniature coke stove was the sole form of heat for both classes, and it wasn't my end either! One just suffered and soldiered on, till finally I got laid low with pneumonia."

As the 1930s progressed the city council introduced senior schools, and St Stephen's head Mr Knights left to take charge of one in Malvern Road in 1934. In 1936 the school's seniors were transferred to the new Samuel Southall School on Merriman's Hill, now Bishop Perowne School, leaving St Stephen's as a junior school.

Mr Daniel took over the headship, to be followed later by Mr Westwood, and plans were made for a new junior school building to house 500 children, but they were dashed by the outbreak, three years later, of WWII.

Many children were evacuated from urban areas and at the start of the autumn term on 11 September the school was occupied by both the St Stephen's pupils and youngsters from Montgomery Street Junior School, Birmingham, with each school getting half a day in the classroom and spending the remaining time organising outdoor activities. The situation was alleviated somewhat by the use of the church hall in Penbury Street.

In 1940 church links with the school were severed after 78 years. The cost to the church of improvements to school buildings that inspectors had been calling for since 1913 could have been substantial. Ironically the improvements had still not been carried out a quarter of a century later.

In 1944 the head of the girls' department of the school, Miss E. Turner, died and the boys' and girls' departments were subsequently amalgamated to create St Stephen's Junior Mixed School.

In 1958 Mr Westwood retired and was succeeded by Mr K.G. Langley who, six years later, presided over centenary celebrations, looking forward to another hundred years and still hoping for that new building which had been the dream of heads for more than 30 years. Sadly it was not to be. The school subsequently closed and flats now stand on the site in Ombersley Road.

Secondary Schools

Some of the city's leading secondary schools are to be found in and around Barbourne. The Royal Grammar School, Worcester, occupying the site in the Upper Tything which was formerly the White Ladies convent, appears to have been founded by Elizabeth I, but it is actually much older, and nor has it been on its present site since Tudor times; it moved there only in 1868.

The almshouses built by the Six Masters governing body of the Royal Grammar School on the site of the White Ladies tythe barn at Little London

The school, associated with the Trinity Guild and the Worcester parish of St Nicholas, was founded at an unknown early date - 685 has even been suggested - and it was first definitely recorded in a document of 1291 when it was known simply as Worcester School.

By the early sixteenth century the Trinity Guild had fallen on hard times and was having difficulty in supporting the school, and the foundation by Henry VIII of the King's School at the cathedral left the grammar school struggling to survive. When, in 1553, the schoolmaster left to make more money elsewhere, the school went into abeyance and remained so for the five years of Mary's reign.

Its fortunes changed in 1558 when Elizabeth came to the throne and Worcester clothier Thomas Wylde gave Pitchcroft to the city as an endowment on condition that the school was re-established. The city appealed to Elizabeth and in 1561 she granted a charter refounding the school and establishing the 'six masters', as the governing body has been known ever since. The school nevertheless remained in a room at St Swithin's Church.

In 1860 Rev Francis John Eld became master of the school, which then had just 30 pupils, and he set about raising standards and improving finances. Five years later he persuaded the six masters to put up £1,000 for a new school and in 1868 Queen Victoria granted a second charter, which accorded the school its

The Physical Laboratory at the Royal Grammer School in 1903

'royal' title, and the governors set about building the present school, which was opened in August 1868, with fees of four guineas (£4.20) a year and by 1877 had 50 pupils.

The site already boasted the range of eighteenth century buildings known as Whiteladies, incorporating part of the chapel of the former convent, which Rev Eld was able to rent initially for £65 a year. Other than that the buildings on the site date from 1868 or later.

In 1898 the school appointed its first lay headmaster in at least 500 years, Frederick A. Hillard MA of Merton College, Oxford. A contemporary described him as having "a strong and vigorous personality" and he set to with a will to improve school buildings and equipment and transform the school's classical curriculum.

Four years on the school was still teaching Latin and Greek, history and geography, but it was also offering modern languages, sciences, craft skills and commercial subjects such as shorthand and technical drawing. As a result, the school doubled in size to 212 pupils, taught by a staff of 10, mostly graduate, masters.

Pupils who have attended the school over the years include the artist Benjamin Williams Leader 1841-45 and in 1852 Adam Lindsay Gordon, Australia's leading nineteenth century poet. The school took Voluntary Aided status under the local education authority in 1949 but reverted to independent status in 1983.

The area also boasted two girls' secondary schools. The first of these to be established was the Worcester High School for Girls, under which name it opened at Britannia House in the Tything in June 1883, though it is better known to us as the Alice Ottley School. Prime mover behind the project was Rev William John Butler, Canon of Worcester, who had a special interest in the education of girls and had already created a school at Wantage when he was vicar there.

Backers formed a company to finance the school, with capital of £5,000 in £50 shares. The Lord Lieutenant of the county, the sixth Earl Beauchamp, headed the governing council of eleven and, within a few months, purchased Britannia House and leased the site and buildings to the school for a nominal rent.

The day and boarding school began with just ten pupils and three assistant mistresses, Miss Crump, Miss Douglas who went on to become head of Godolphin High School, Salisbury in 1899, and Miss Perks who taught music and singing at the school for many years, under the direction of the first headmistress, 43-year-old Alice Ottley.

Miss Ottley was the third of twelve children of a Yorkshire vicar and the sister of a bishop and had no formal education or training as a teacher, but was said to have gained her first experience bringing up a tribe of younger brothers and sisters. When her father died in 1861 the family moved to Hampstead and she helped her mother to open a school for girls. In the early days of the Cambridge

Local Examinations she obtained a certificate in honours with five distinctions.

She subsequently gained experience in a girls' school at Brondesbury, famous in its day, before being appointed to the new school in Worcester, where she had furnished rooms, a salary of £250 a year and £1 a head for every girl on roll over 150.

The tuition fees were not small, varying from one to five guineas (£1.05p - £5.25p) a term, but within a year the numbers had shot up from 10 to 87, in two years to 125, by March 1892 to 171 and by summer 1897 to 205.

In 1892 the first university degree was achieved by an 'old girl', a BA (London) awarded to Miss S. Sitwell, and three years later Miss M.A. Hogarth **Alice Ottley in 1881** achieved the school's first university scholarship, to Lady Margaret Hall, Oxford. In 1903 the Worcester Daily Times called the school "the leading educational establishment for young ladies in the city and county".

The head was regarded as being responsible for this desirable state of affairs. Her quiet, studious, enthusiasm for "her children" inspired affection and respect in the staff and girls, while she exhibited meticulous attention to detail and unfail-

The first staff and pupils of the then Worcester High School for Girls in 1883

ingly encouraged the same high standards in others that she expected of herself. Her biographer, Mary James, noted approvingly that Miss Ottley's letters, even in her last days, were impeccably written; "she always insisted on accurate punctuation", said Miss James. The head was also keen on physical education. The girls played their first tennis match against Oxford High School in 1894, the year in which the school also began hockey matches. They had played cricket four years earlier against Edgbaston High School, but by the 1920s it was noted that the sport was restricted to girls under 15. The school had a gymnasium by 1904 and a science laboratory by 1910.

In 1898 the death of the school's benefactor, Lord Beauchamp, who had provided its premises, precipitated a crisis. If the school's premises had been sold there might have been a danger that it would close. Fortunately wealthy backers were once more found, including John Corbett, the 'salt king' of Droitwich who built the Chateau Impney, and the premises were purchased for the school at a cost of £17,388.

After 29 years as head, Alice Ottley retired due to ill health in June 1912, aged 72, and she died in that same year on 18 September, the day that the school assembled for the first time under her successor. At her funeral at Worcester Cathedral, Canon Claughton said: "No other person has during the last thirty years contributed so much to the highest spiritual good of this city". She was buried at Astwood Cemetary.

To honour her role in building the school into the respected educational institution it had become, the governing council renamed it Alice Ottley School. Fifty-seven years later, in 1969, the Warwickshire and Worcestershire Life magazine noted: "the school is an oasis of educational calm (which) presents a picture of the old-fashioned virtues of discipline, good manners and tidiness"; it sounded very much as if Alice Ottley would still approve of her school.

The area's other girls' school, and the only one of the secondaries actually in Barbourne, was the Worcester Grammar School for Girls, though it also originally had a different name.

It apparently began life in 1896 at the Victoria Institute, which housed a technical school providing secondary education for local youngsters and, for a few years, a more advanced Organised Science School, a boys' day school under principal Mr J.A. Cooper. Local historian Ron Shuard, who has researched the history of the girls' grammar, believes girls were also catered for there.

The school was not very successful and closed in 1908. The boys then went to the grammar school in the Tything, but for the girls a new school was founded, Worcester Secondary School for Girls, which had 80 girls on the first day, taught by headmistress Miss Steel and four mistresses.

The school continued to use the Victoria Institute as its base, but this was not a very successful arrangement, since the only space available was the lecture theatre and workshops in the basement, used by carpentry and engineering students in the evenings. So further building work went ahead and in 1910 the girls moved into their own rooms on the site. Not only did they now have their own entrance in Taylor's Lane, but for the first time, every form had its own room and every girl had her own desk.

Numbers rose quickly, and in 1920 the city purchased Thames House on the corner of Barbourne Terrace which was occupied initially by the upper sixth form. Thames House was subsequently demolished and in 1928 work began on the three-acre site to build a new school which opened in the following year.

There was accommodation in the new building for 400 girls, but this was always a popular and successful school and by 1945 numbers had increased to 476. In that year the school was renamed the City of Worcester Grammar School for Girls.

The numbers continued to rise and in 1962 the school moved to a new building in Spetchley Road which later became Worcester Sixth Form College. Bishop Perowne School, named for a former bishop of Worcester, subsequently occupied the Thames House site for some years before moving to the former Samuel Southall site on Merrimans Hill Road. The Thames House site now houses an annexe of Worcester College of Technology.

The Second World War

Barbourne went to war in 1939, along with the rest of Britain. The city council was active in building air raid shelters in school grounds, including St George's, usually of brick with a concrete roof, and public shelters of similar construction were built on many streets. Shelters were also created at the hospitals, not forgetting the Eye Hospital on Barbourne Road, and many pubs built shelters for their patrons.

Petrol tankers parked overnight on a tree-lined track on the east side of Pitchcroft, so that they had some cover in the event of air attack. Part of Pitchcroft was also reportedly used for growing wheat. To deter any attempts by the enemy to land on open areas of Pitchcroft old tram tracks were erected there as aircraft landing obstacles, and in case of air attack with chemical weapons, the gymnasium at the Royal Grammar School was fitted out as a decontamination centre. The school was also designated as a centre of resistance in the event of invasion and military operations would have been directed from there.

Concrete pillboxes sprang up at the Droitwich Road/Ombersley Road junction and at the end of Farrier Street. The old water works, which was also designated a 'centre of resistance' and had a sandbagged machine gun post at the entrance, was the HQ of No.1 Platoon of the 1st Battalion, Worcestershire Home

Boy scouts recycling for victory in the yard of The Talbot in Barbourne, in this war-time picture, courtesy of the Worcester News. Fourth from left is Martin Smith of St George's scouts, whose dad was driving the lorry, but the collection was made by Claines scouts

Guard, and the old water tower was used as an observation point.

The WVS, who kept everyone going with tea and buns, had their HQ over what was then a music shop at 59 & 60, the Tything, and the air raid wardens based themselves in a wooden school cricket pavilion at Pound Walk.

Fire was always a risk from air raids and there were fire watchers based in strategic locations such as the roof of the Labour Exchange in Castle Street, beside the end of Love's Grove, and on the tower of Spreckley's Brewery off Barbourne Road, where residents with long memories have told us there was also a Home Guard arms store on the ground floor. Metal water tanks for use by the fire brigade were placed in a number of streets.

In case air raids should cut off road and rail links, emergency food stores were placed in strategic locations around the city, ready to issue supplies to the local population if necessary. Possibly the last of these left standing is the large corrugated iron building next to the church opposite the end of York Place, though there is some doubt about whether this appeared until later in the war. The Odeon cinema in Foregate Street, of which only the shell had been built when war broke out, was used for storage of aircraft parts.

This building in Albany Terrace may be the last WWII emergency food store left standing in the city, though there is some doubt about when it was built

Perhaps Barbourne's greatest contribution to the war effort was the production of a factory apparently so secret that its presence was completely unknown to wartime residents. It was reportedly secreted in a residential area near to the bottom of York Place, where a private housing development for the elderly now stands.

In wartime this was said to be part of a network of 'shadow factories' which the government secretly set up in residential areas, with the intention of hiding them from enemy air attacks. The location was finally revealed in 1996 to researchers for the Defence of Britain project, conducted by archaeologists to discover information about wartime sites. They were led to the site by a former wartime air raid warden, who would have needed to know the location of such sites as part of his job.

The factory was apparently part of Windshields, a local company now defunct but formerly based at Gregory's Mill, making vehicle windscreens in peacetime. During the war, production of the York Place factory was said to have included turret and cockpit canopies for Lancaster bombers. The factory was apparently so secret that several wartime York Place residents have told us they knew nothing of it, and a press appeal for information during the preparation of this book produced no response.

The manager of this facility was said to have lodged during war-time at a large house at the end of Albany Terrace, but we could find no trace of anyone who remembered him. With the informant who brought this factory to light now sadly dead, and Windshields long since out of business, we had little to go on when we started our search for this important site.

The Ministry of Aircraft Production factory, described in the Defence of Britain project details as square and well-lit with plenty of windows, was said to be in York Place but there was nowhere in this residential street where such a factory could have been sited. The only open land was immediately to the north of the end of the street, and during the war it was a smallholding run by Jim Bennett who lived in the street.

However a lady who was born in York Place in 1915 and has lived all her life there, pointed out to us the site nearby of buildings which were standing during the war. She had no knowledge of the shadow factory, but the site which she identified, at the end of Leicester Street, beyond Whistone Terrace, seems the only possible location for this facility.

These buildings later housed a bowling green and a company named Worcester Woodcraft, but the site was taken over by Metal Box in the 1950s and a new factory was built there. An Ordnance Survey map of 1940 shows a substantial building on the site, some 156 feet in length and 65 feet wide, stretching from the frontages of properties in Whistone Terrace, Leicester Street, almost to the rear of properties in Ashcroft Road.

The building was described simply as a 'Club', though if it was a secret aircraft components factory it would hardly be marked as such on a publicly-available map. A map of 1970 shows a building of somewhat different dimensions on

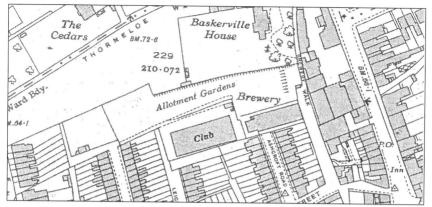

The 'club' in the centre of this 1940 Ordnance Survey map may have been the site identified as a secret WWII aircraft components factory

the same site, described as an 'engineering works'. The Metal Box factory was empty for some years before it was demolished and the present housing development built.

It seems likely that it was in the vanished war-time buildings that the aircraft parts factory which helped keep wartime Lancasters in the air was situated, but there is no absolute certainty of this. It appears that the veil of secrecy with which these factories were inevitably shrouded is still protecting the location of Barbourne's shadow factory 60 years on, and we may never know for certain exactly where it was located.

APPENDICES

Appendix A - The 904 Charter

The original 904 charter, containing the first recorded reference to Barbourne, has not survived, nor apparently has any copy in Worcester; the only two surviving copies are both in the Cotton manuscripts in the British Library, referenced Nero E i pt. 2 fo. 182 and Tiberius A xiii fos. 6v-7v.

The Tiberius charter was one of a series of copies made and bound together in the early eleventh century, possibly as early as 1016. The pages are a little larger than A5 in size with a text area roughly 100mm wide by 190mm high. These were long regarded as the work of the Worcester monk Hemming who made a compilation of the bishop's charters for Bishop Wulstan later in the eleventh century, but analysis of handwriting and textual evidence has since proved that to be incorrect and the scribe is not known. (For a discussion of this and other issues relating to this charter see *Hemming's Cartulary* by Neil Ripley Ker in *Studies in Medieval History Presented to Frederick Maurice Powicke*, OUP 1948.) There is no means of checking whether the charter in Cotton Tiberius is an accurate copy of the original but scholars regard these manuscripts as of good quality and a sound source.

The Nero manuscript was one of a series of charters copied and abbreviated from the Tiberius manuscripts onto large folios and ordered by Bishop Wulstan to be bound in the great bible presented to Worcester by King Offa. This was obviously regarded as a safe place to keep important charters, but the copying was inaccurate which has led to them being regarded by scholars as worthless. Unfortunately however, staining has partly obliterated the wording of the Tiberius charter and it is presumably for that reason that a number of authors who have published transcripts or translation of this charter have chosen to use the Nero manuscript. For some purposes this may not cause problems, but in relation to Barbourne, Tiberius contains important information which is not included in Nero.

The earliest published version of the charter was a transcript of the original Latin and Anglo-Saxon in Cartularium Saxonicum, Ed. Bruce (pp. 266-7), published 1887. The first translation, and the only parallel Latin-Anglo-Saxon/English version published, appeared in A.J. Robertson's Anglo-Saxon Charters (Cambridge, 2nd. ed. 1956, pp. 35-8) while a partial translation appeared in Della Hooke's Worcestershire Anglo-Saxon Charter-bounds (Boydell Press 1990 pp. 241-3). All these published versions were based on the Nero manuscript and none contained a reference to 'Ludading wic', the farmstead or holding of the Ludadinga tribe, which is found only in the Tiberius manuscript, though Miss Robertson included it in a footnote as a reference which she was unable to explain. The translation used here is from A.E.E. Jones's book Anglo-Saxon Worcester (1958, pp. 98-100) which refers to Bruce, based on Nero, but appears to provide a compilation of material from both the manuscript versions of the charter, and from our point of view therefore is the most complete translation available.

Grant of land to Duke Ethelred and his wife Ethelflaede by
Bishop Werefrith of Worcester in St Clement's Parish each
side of river and at Barbourne (Ludading Wic)

Forasmuch as it is well-known and clearly established among all wise folk that the words or deeds of men, by reason of manifold confusion caused by tribulations, and by reason of the wandering of thoughts, frequently slip from memory, unless they are preserved and recalled to memory by being set down in writing and by the precaution of being entrusted to written records, therefore, for this reason in the 904th year of Our Lord's incarnation, we have ordered it to be written for the sake of the memory of posterity.

Namely that Bishop Werefrith and the Chapter at Worcester give and bestow on Aethelred and Aethelflaed their lords, the enclosure within the city walls of Worcester which is from the river itself by the north wall eastward 28 rods long and then to the south 24 rods broad, and then again westwards along to the Severn 18 rods long. And also we give them that pasture land on the west of the Severn opposite the messuage and along the Bishop's Dyke from the river eye (an island or sand bar which existed in the Severn at that time), so that it comes west out from Moor Dyke and so north out opposite the eye and so eastwards that it comes again to the Severn below the eye. Also, we give them Ludading Wic by Barbourne [Bever Brook], and in addition 60 acres of arable land to the south of Bever Brook, and another 60 to the north and very generously 12 acres besides of good pasture land. They give all to them for their mercy and desire that they, and also their servants and their church, be friends of their lord. And they will intercede with God day and night for reward to them for this as best they may. And Ethelred and Ethelfleda shall hold it for all time; both within and without the town wall—uncontested by anyone as long as they live. And if Elfwine survives them it shall similarly remain uncontested as long as she lives, and after the death of all three it shall be given back without dispute to the lord of the church for the souls of the three of them, endowed as it then—if it be God's will, that they may endow it.

May those who enrich and guard it be enriched by the reward of everlasting happiness in Heaven, and may those who diminish and break it be confounded by everlasting censure, unless they first make amends with proper satisfaction. This Charter all the Chapter, young and old, confirmed with the sign of the Cross of Christ, and the twelve names of them written below, also the names of the friends we chose as witnesses for us.

Ethelred—Ethelflaed—Werfrith B—Kenelm [Abbot of Evesham]—Ecgfrith [Pbr]—Wiglaf [Pbr]—Oslac [Pbr]—Cinath [Deacon]—Bernhelm—Eardwulf—Wlfred—Coelhelm—Wllfa—Alhmound—Edgar [B]—Aldred—Ethelfrid—Alderman—Alfred —Alfstan—Eadric—Wlfhun.

A3.

Appendix B - A Note on Population Statistics

Data on population in Part Two of this book, on the development of modern Barbourne, is based on tables in the Victoria County History of Worcestershire (Vol 4), for population levels in all parishes in the county throughout the nineteenth century.

Barbourne was not however a civil parish in its own right and its population figures are therefore included within Claines parish; subsumed within those of the wider rural parish and those urban areas of the parish which took in other parts of north Worcester apart from Barbourne.

Claines parish statistics were in fact split into five different categories, three of which were included in the city of Worcester. Fortunately one set of these statistics, referring to part of the township of Claines within the city, can be identified as comparable to the chapelry of St George, which was identified in a map of 1861 as broadly covering the area between Castle Street and the brook. This map identified the parish bounds accorded to the chapelry from 1862 but these bounds seem likely to be comparable to the chapelry bounds from 1830.

In addition, the Tything area was shown separately in statistics and a map of c. 1830 shows the Tything bounds coverering the area from Castle Street to roughly where Shrubbery Avenue is situated today, so the statistics for the township or chapelry must logically relate to the chapelry bounds minus the Tything area. The statistics for the township or chapelry within the city should therefore provide reasonably accurate population figures for Barbourne as it was throughout much of the nineteenth century and all figures for Barbourne population during this period are taken from the Claines Township included within Worcester.

The VCH statistics are based on the 1841 standard and therefore are not affected by, and could be said to anticipate, the political boundary changes which took place during the nineteenth century.

Appendix C Dating of Streets in and around Barbourne 1730 - 1908

The dates shown here are the earliest found.   To obtain dating evidence we have checked maps, planning records, street directories and a variety of documentary sources. Despite this we cannot be certain that some streets may not have existed earlier than the dates given here and many certainly existed as unnamed lanes or tracks long before they became the streets and roads we know today. Equally many streets were not complete when first listed and further houses were subsequently built. The streets listed here are only those which are to be found in available street directories up to 1908. Where the first mention is DS, M or similar source the first known directory entry is also noted.

Abbreviations :   BD -   Bentley's Directory of Worcestershire
                  DS -   Documentary sources
                  LD -   Littlebury's Directory
                  M -   Included on a map of the date shown
                  PA -   Planning application
                  PB -   Percy, Butcher & Co's Directory of Worcester
                  PO -   Post Office Directory
                  SG -   Stanley's Worcester and Malvern Guide Book
                  WRD - Worcester Royal Directory

Name	Date	Source	Notes
Albany Terrace	1830s	DS	1842 BD
Alma Street	1874	PB	As Lane: Street 1884 LD
Ashcroft Road	1905	LD	
Back Lane	1880	LD	
Back Walk	1874	PB	
Barbourne (Road)	1790	WRD	As Barbourne: Rd 1896 LD
Barbourne Lane	1851	SG	1874 PB
Barbourne Terrace	1759	DS	1842 BD
Barbourne Walk	1880	LD	
Berkeley Street	1896	LD	
Blanquettes Street	1896	LD	
Bourne Street	1896	LD	"Newly formed"
Brewery Walk	1896	LD	
Britannia Place	1842	BD	
Britannia Road	1874	PB	
Britannia Square	1820s	DS	1842 BD
Britannia Place	1842	PB	
Bromsgrove Street	1880	LD	
Brook Street	1896	LD	

Chestnut Walk	1842	BD	
Chestnut Row	1874	PB	
Chestnut Place	1874	PB	
Chestnut Street	1874	PB	
Crown Street	1880	LD	As Lane: Street 1884 LD
Cumberland Street	1874	PB	
Cypress Street	1896	LD	
Flag Meadow Walk	1896	LD	
Gregory's Bank	1830	M	1896 LD
Gregory's Mill Street	1896	LD	Mill Lane 1874 PB
Hebb Street	1896	LD	
Henry Street	1896	LD	
Ivy Street	1885	LD	
Lansdowne Street	1874	PB	
Lavender Road	1884	LD	
Leicester Street	1908	LD	
Little London	1851	DS	1874 PB
Lyttelton Street	1896	LD	
Melbourne Street	1896	LD	
Melbourne Terrace	1874	PB	
Mill Lane	1874	PB	
New Bank Street	1874	PB	
Northcote Street	1896	LD	
Northwick Lane	1874	PB	
Northwick Road	1880	LD	
Northwick Terrace	1874	PB	
Offley Street	1905	LD	
Old Northwick (Lane)	1884	LD	
Paradise Place	1864	PO	
Paradise Row	1864	PO	Eighteenth century
Park Avenue	1896	LD	
Park View Terrace	1896	LD	
Perdiswell Street	1884	LD	
Pinkett Street	1884	M	1885 LD
Pitchcroft Lane	1884	M	1885 LD
Pope Iron Road	1896	LD	
Price Street	1896	LD	
Raglan Street	1884	LD	
Redcliffe Street	1896	LD	
Sandys Road	1874	PB	
Selborne Road	1896	LD	

Sharman Road	1896	LD	
Saunders Street	1896	LD	
Shrubbery Avenue	c.1894	DS	1896 LD
Shrubbery Road	1908	LD	
Somers Road	1884	LD	
Somerset Place	1896	LD	
Stephenson Terrace	1864	PO	1896 LD
St George's Lane North	1835	DS	Scl 1835:1851 SG: 1874 PB: N 1880 LD
St George's Lane South	1884	LD	
St George's Square	1820s	DS	1842 BD
St Oswald's Road	1874	PB	
St Stephen's Place	1874	PB	
St Stephen's Street	1896	LD	
St Stephen's Terrace	1880	LD	
Summer Street	1896	LD	As Place 1874 PB
Sunnyside Road	1905	LD	
Tennis Walk	1885	LD	
The Tything	1842	BD	
Thorneloe Road	1874	PB	
Thorneloe Walk	1896	LD	
Tower Road	1896	LD	
Townsend Street	1896	LD	
Turrall Street	1884	LD	
Victoria Street	1896	LD	
Vine Street	1896	LD	
Wakeman Street	1896	LD	
Waterworks Road	1884	LD	
White Ladies Close	1874	PB	
Woodbine Road	1896	LD	
York Place	1835	DS	1842 BD